Coding for Beginners: Blockchain Development

A step-by-step guide to create your own Blockchains, Cryptocurrencies and NFTs

By

Elliot Davis

BEFORE YOU START READING, DOWNLOAD YOUR FREE DIGITAL ASSETS!

Be sure to visit the URL below on your computer or mobile device to access the free digital asset files that are included with your purchase of this book.

These digital assets will complement the material in the book and are referenced throughout the text.

DOWNLOAD YOURS HERE:

https://codeconnections.net/#newsletter

Table of Content

Introduction

The world as we know it is powered by coding, although most people are unaware of its capabilities. Regardless of what it is, coding is critical for most of today's enterprises.

Coding powers our digital world forward. Every website, mobile application, computer program, calculator, and even microwave depends on code to function. It is surprising to know how many people are still unaware of how coding works and its role in our modern world. The latest innovation in the financial world is cryptocurrency, a complex code construction. Transactions are carried out through different platforms developed by coding and have no physical existence. Still, they have changed the way people look at currency, trading, and business transactions in the digital marketplace and is making its way into the physical marketplace.

This book is a great introduction to the technology known as Blockchain. According to some, the Blockchain will accomplish for transactions what the Internet accomplished for information. This means that it has the power to enhance efficiency and trust in every transaction of goods or services. The Blockchain has the potential to alter how the world operates fundamentally. If you have ever purchased a home, you are likely to have had to sign a large stack of documents from different stakeholders to complete the transaction. If you have ever registered a vehicle, you are probably aware of how inconvenient the procedure may be. Many people want to know more about programming and blockchains, but they cannot find a book that gives the precise and to-the-point instructions to keep them engaged. This book aims to provide both, a learning platform that targets beginners of coding.

This book is for those who want to learn to code but have little to no knowledge about how to create apps and programs, or they may participate in the latest form of finance and technology- cryptocurrency. This book serves as a guide for all.

I have been trading for nearly a decade, and nothing has captured my attention more than the rising cryptocurrency technology. I devote most of my time and resources to studying how digital currencies and cryptocurrency mechanisms function and how these new currencies might be used to benefit individuals in today's financial world. I have been in the cryptocurrency business for the better part of a decade at the time of writing this. Being involved in crypto research and blockchain development has put me in a position of authority and expertise to teach people who are interested in this new technology. As for coding and development, I have always been passionate about it, and I have attended numerous coding courses throughout the years to improve my skills. I have failed numerous times along the way to understand the obstacles that new comers may face on their journeys and have discovered the best strategies for overcoming these obstacles.

This book aims to provide an interesting, enjoyable, and straightforward introduction to Blockchain and Blockchain development through a breakdown of basic coding and programming concepts. By the end of this book, readers will have a working knowledge of Blockchain concepts by creating their own cryptocurrency and NFT and also delving deeper into the idea of Decentralized Apps or DApps by using different programming languages. Blockchain technology, which is most simply described as a shared, immutable ledger, can revolutionize how the modern world handles transactions. To be clear, when I discuss Blockchain, I am not referring to bitcoin.

I am referring to the underlying digital infrastructure that allows applications such as bitcoin to work. To be clear, the Blockchain's reach extends well beyond bitcoin.

Some terminologies require technical knowledge of information technology. However, this is not required for this book. To avoid confusion, this book uses everyday English, and it will walk you through the process of how digital money was created and how you can learn to code and develop your own blockchains, cryptos, or NFTs.

To help with comprehension, we will briefly review history of finance and then explain what brought about the formation of many cryptocurrencies in today's society. Following that, we will examine the ideas and motivations of the Bitcoin inventor Satoshi Nakamoto. Then, in further detail, we will examine the various contenders for the birth father of Blockchain. We will also discuss how each block is formed and how they eventually form a chain, which we refer to as Blockchain.

In the last chapters, we will discuss the security measures implemented on the Blockchain further in depth. We will then examine why this technology will transform the world by examining commercial applications and future banking systems. Finally, a summary of what the Blockchain is in a nutshell.

While blockchain technology is as robust as the Internet, it stores identical data blocks across its network, in contrast to the Web2 Internet of today. As a result, a blockchain cannot be centralized or have a single point of failure. By distributing data across its network, the Blockchain eliminates the risks associated with centrally stored data. Blockchain networks lack centralized points of vulnerability that computer hackers can easily exploit.

Everybody is familiar with the security issues that afflict today's Internet. To access our online assets, we all rely on username and password credentials. Blockchain technology enhances security by utilizing encryption technology. By enabling the widespread distribution of data and information, blockchain technology has established the backbone of the new Internet, Web3. Though Blockchain was initially developed for the digital currency Bitcoin, the business and technology communities are discovering a plethora of uses for it. Not only programmers, but all businesses, will require knowledge of this new technology. Blockchain will fundamentally alter business models across all industries — and may even alter how people work and live.

As a company the Code Connections team has been involved in computing technology since 1974 when it made its first practical appearance on Wall Street. We have used and written about a variety of evolving technology tools, from IBM Assemblers, Fortran, COBOL, and data access methods such as QSAM, BDAM, and VSAM to modern REST web services, Java, and SQL, and everything in between (including client/server tools such as PowerBuilder). We have been fortunate that our enthusiasm for learning and becoming proficient in each new and emerging technology has served us well in the business world. We have recognized blockchain technology as an ingenious invention because it combines the best of previous database design, cryptography, and virtual machine container technology with today's extremely capable distributed computing environment. Our enthusiasm for technology stems from a case of love at first sight. We have assembled a strong network of blockchain entrepreneurs, fellow blockchain technologists, and others who have contributed significantly to this book's content and text.

This book is intended for anyone interested in blockchain technology and its applications. It is also useful to anyone designing a blockchain application—which is necessary to create solutions in this domain. Furthermore, online and application developers at all levels and tech-savvy businesses interested in staying current on technology in general and Blockchain, in particular, will find the talks in this book informative.

The book discusses the definition of Blockchain, use cases, distributed technology, and, most importantly, blockchain development, with code snippets and recommended practices. It focuses on the Ethereum blockchain, introducing Solidity and other Ethereum framework components. Also, it covers the setup, development, validation, and deployment of a fully-featured blockchain application or a stand-alone program.

Interest in coding has increased in recent years. Worldwide, schools are incorporating coding into their curriculum, code clubs are forming to teach newcomers, and adults are returning to college to acquire the skills increasingly deemed essential in the industry. And millions of individuals throughout the world are learning to code for the sheer joy of it.

Fortunately, there has never been a more favorable time to begin learning to code. Historically, programmers had to manually enter each line of code, employing arcane commands and mathematical symbols. A single misplaced full stop might devastate the entire composition. Today, using drag-and-drop coding languages such as ScratchTM, you can create astonishingly powerful programs in minutes.

As learning to code has become more accessible, society has become aware of computers' creative potential, which is where this book comes in.

Each chapter in the book is self-contained, focusing on a specific area of blockchain technology and its applications. The chapters are structured to build on the preceding one to create a sound conceptual knowledge of Blockchain. This is supplemented by a full overview of getting started as a blockchain application designer and developer.

We will discuss programming and coding in the first chapter of the book to give you an overview of how these systems work.

Chapter 1: The Fundamentals

The first chapter of this book will discuss the basic fundamentals of coding and cryptocurrency. To understand the concept of blockchains and cryptocurrency, it is very important to understand how computer programming works.

Now, coding is not a very complex field of work and can be understood if one gives proper time and dedication to the subject. To understand in-depth coding concepts, we need to learn a bit about what a program is. But first, let's go through a brief overview of Bitcoin & Blockchains

1.1 History of Bitcoin

Bitcoin can be broadly classified as a "digital currency." Bitcoin functions similarly to traditional forms of money in many ways, except that there is no physical money, and all transactions take place exclusively through the Internet. Different digital currencies are available, but Bitcoin is now the most popular, highly valued, and widely utilized.

As we dive deeper, it will be beneficial to consider Bitcoin in two contexts: a currency and a technology. Later in this book, we discuss the groundbreaking technology that underpins Bitcoin. For the time being though, let us consider Bitcoin as a currency and learn a little about its history.

Bitcoin Beginnings

It is truly superior to any superhero origin narrative, as it is entirely factual. This origin story is true and within our own universe!

Satoshi Nakamoto, a mysterious individual, published an online paper titled "Bitcoin: A Peer-to-Peer Electronic Cash System" in 2008. He described his vision for a new kind of electronic money in it. Consider a world in which transmitting money to other individuals is as simple as sending an email.

Electronic money had been attempted previously but had typically failed due to the ease of copying anything over the Internet; you can see this in examples like music files, films, and confidential government data. To create trustworthy and secure digital cash, Satoshi's vision was to combine a number of new technologies — cryptography, peer-to-peer file sharing, and blockchain.

He referred to it as bitcoin.

Bitcoin is the most well-known blockchain initiative; it is a type of "digital money" that enables users to send money as easily as they send a text message.

Nobody knew who Satoshi was, but no one cared since after all it was the Internet. Over the next two years, he expanded the bitcoin technology, enlisting the assistance of a small group of programmers to test, build, and refine it. They were compensated for their efforts on the project with small sums of bitcoin, which were worth nothing at the time but a bit bragging rights.

Satoshi was never found, as he interacted solely through internet forums and email. Meanwhile, the bitcoin network increased in size and strength. As with the Internet, bitcoin operated on a shared network of computers, with "miners" rewarded for contributing computational power to the network with little quantities of bitcoin that were still worthless except for bragging rights at that moment.

This established a vicious cycle: miners were suddenly "paid" in bitcoin, which created an incentive to contribute additional processing power because who knows what might happen if this bitcoin becomes valuable one day?

Satoshi toiled away in the background, correcting issues, offering improvements, and herding the cats. However, no one ever met him in person. In 2010, Satoshi began distributing all of the source code to his developers, heightening the mystery.

And then he vanished.

He left many personal bitcoin accounts containing at least one million bitcoins, worth more than 19 billion dollars seven years later. And he never returned to retrieve it.

Who is responsible for this? Who develops a life-changing technology and then vanishes, leaving wealth behind?

The nature of bitcoin is such that others can see what he has in his account, much like a transparent bank vault but cannot access it without his permission. Additionally, because no bank "holds" bitcoin, Satoshi can remain safely anonymous. His unclaimed money is trapped in time.

Bitcoin devotees have gone insane in their pursuit of Satoshi's identity. From conspiracy theorists to language experts, everyone has combed over every letter he ever sent, attempting to deduce his ethnicity or even just his time zone.

In 2014, Newsweek believed it had a scoop when it discovered a guy named Dorian Satoshi Nakamoto residing in California. (He vehemently denied it.) Even the world's leading investigative journalists were baffled. Perhaps Satoshi was a female, a group, a government or extraterrestrials! Nobody knows for certain.

Bitcoin was the "explosion" that triggered the Blockchain Revolution. Satoshi may have vanished, but his creation is wreaking havoc on the world.

Bitcoin as a form of currency

When we consider Bitcoin as a currency or a digital asset, there are two significant questions that most people immediately ask:

How is the Bitcoin value determined?

How is it used in practice?

To address the first question, we have to consider paper money, such as US dollars. When pressed, there is little physical difference between a $100 bill and a scrap of paper. A hundred-dollar bill is perceived as more than a piece of paper because citizens have come to accept it as having a designated value that can be exchanged for goods and services. Numerous elements contribute to a society's agreement, but in a nutshell, every currency has value because a sufficient number of people agree that it does.

The same is true for Bitcoin. Bitcoin's worth is determined by the number of people ready to accept it as payment, a rapidly expanding group. If no one is ready to accept Bitcoin as a form of currency, it is an undesired possession, nobody wants it, and it becomes worthless. However, as evidence by the price of Bitcoin, it is used and has value. As with other commodities, the price of Bitcoin is controlled by the relationship between supply and demand. As demand increases, the price of Bitcoin climbs as well, and vice versa.

What is the primary purpose of bitcoin?

Bitcoin can be used in the same way any other conventional currency, such as US dollars or Euros. You may use Bitcoin to send and receive payments, make purchases, or even save BTC for future usage. Bitcoin can also be viewed as an investment, much like a stock.

Have you ever used your credit card to make an online transaction or transferred money electronically between accounts? When it comes to transacting with Bitcoin, the method is quite similar in practice. We can make purchases by moving a specified quantity of Bitcoin directly between two accounts, from buyer to seller.

Currently, Bitcoin may be used to purchase a wide variety of items, but not everything. To make a purchase with Bitcoin, you must first find a vendor willing to accept it as payment. Numerous well-known companies, like Subway, Microsoft, OkCupid, Whole Foods, Etsy, and Overstock.com, already accept Bitcoin.

New merchants from a diverse variety of industries are constantly adding Bitcoin payment alternatives. As more people worldwide become involved in the Bitcoin economy, retailers are responding to the growing demand from customers to take Bitcoin.

How is Bitcoin unique?

One of the greatest hurdles of entry for Bitcoin is that many people struggle with the concept of a non-physical currency. When we consider traditional currencies ("fiat") such as the US Dollar or the Euro, we frequently envision paper money. Many of us are accustomed to thinking of money in terms of cash as something physical that we carry around.

However, the majority of people don't carry around sacks of cash. The majority of our money is held in banks. Why is this the case?

While paper money has been used for a long time, it is not very practical in the long run. It is easily lost, stolen, or damaged. Additionally, there is nothing that connects a single piece of paper money to a specific individual.

If you stuff your entire life savings beneath your mattress and get robbed, nothing in the money will identify you as the owner. Unless the authorities apprehend the robber, the money is almost certainly lost forever. This vulnerability is largely why we rely on banks to store the majority of our money for us. Banks provide security in exchange for fees and control the money we store in our bank accounts.

Banks have historically been the only choice for customers to store their currency in a secure, centralized location backed by a guarantee. However, are banks truly the best solution to the problem of money storage?

Banks can restrict, limit, and manage our access to our money based on various variables. For instance, we may be prohibited from withdrawing more than a specified sum at any particular time. We may be charged a large transaction fee while transferring funds across our various accounts. If a bank gets hacked, it can damage millions of accounts, as everything is housed in a single database. Ultimately, despite the numerous drawbacks, most of us end up depositing our money in banks since there is no better choice. We are forced to rely on these banks or risk tucking cash beneath our mattresses.

Bitcoin, in contrast to traditional currencies, is decentralized. Peer-to-peer transactions occur without the intervention of a "middle man" such as a bank, government agency, or other third-party institution. As a result, Bitcoin and many other cryptocurrencies are frequently referred to as "trustless," implying that we can conduct transactions without placing our trust in another party or a financial institution.

1.2 What is Coding?

A common language must exist to enable humans to communicate and create tasks that computers can perform. Computer sciences' history began with the search for a universal language. Humans are already familiar with a variety of specific codes. One such example is the color code used by an electronics student to identify the amount of resistance of a particular resistor. Alphabetic codes have been created for communication purposes. The Morse code used by telegraphers and the semaphore code used for maritime communication are notable examples. Various devices, such as the parity bit, are incorporated into these codes to increase the speed and reliability of its communications.

When viewed through the lens of a coder, one may observe how coding has evolved in a variety of "Editor's Introduction" scenarios. "Why do offspring look like their parents?" is a fundamental question in biology. The genetic code serves as the transmission route, as almost all organisms store descriptions of important proteins in a sequence of triplets. Variations on this fundamental idea enable us to account for the immune response, mutations, and a variety of other biological events.

Coding can also take place in the bodily form. The messages used to represent a sensation can be sampled in a variety of ways. The nervous system is responsible for transmitting information from one portion of the body to another. Additionally, coding is used throughout the animal world. Bees' code for communicating the location of a food source is arguably the best-known example of insect coding.

A machine is only capable of comprehending two forms of data: off and on. Indeed, a computer is nothing more than a collection of "on/off" switches, commonly referred to as transistors.

Anything a computer can do, results from a unique combination of some switches being turned on and some switches being turned off.

Binary code represents these combinations as 0s and 1s, with each digit representing a single switch. Bytes are groupings of eight digits that indicate eight switches in binary code, for example, 11001101. Modern computers generate millions, if not billions, of switches, resulting in an incomprehensibly large number of possible configurations.

However, there is one caveat here. To create a computer program by writing billions of 1s and 0s will require superhuman abilities, and even if successful, it will take a lifetime or more.

This is why programming languages are necessary.

We can create computer applications, mobile applications, and websites using hundreds of different programming languages. Rather than binary code, such as 01010, they let us produce relatively easy code to read, write, and comprehend. Each language requires unique software to convert the data we add into binary code that a machine can understand.

Numerous languages have been developed to assist programmers with specific goals in mind - some are useful for web development, some for desktop application development, and others for numerical and scientific problems.

There are two sorts of programming languages: low-level and high-level.

Low-level languages bear a greater resemblance to the binary code (for example, 01101) that computers understand, whereas high-level languages bear a considerably less resemblance to binary code. High-level languages are easier to program because they are less difficult and designed to be straightforward for users to write.

Almost all of today's popular programming languages are high-level languages.

Now, before I get more into the fundamentals of coding, allow me to illustrate how beneficial it may be for you.

1.3 What is a Program?

A program is a set of instructions intended to be executed by humans or intelligent machines.

We are primarily concerned with the instructions that a computer program issues to a digital computer. The program may be quite basic, requiring only the input of a few statements and their output in alphabetical order, or it may be rather sophisticated, requiring branch points and convergence criteria to determine when it is complete. Computer programs must be written in a computer language that is both human and computer-readable. Computer language development is as an important topic as is linguistics — the study of languages and their grammars.

1.4 A Brief Introduction to Programming

In general, programming is a collection of instructions that the computer uses to perform specific tasks. This is also referred to as coding. Before getting into an in-depth discussion, it is necessary to understand how programming works and how the computer processes instructions. It becomes relatively simple to construct functions, operators, and syntax for any language when you understand how to write computer programs correctly. Additionally, programming communicates with computers via binary language, requiring programmers to comprehend high-level and low-level languages and syntax.

Solving Problems Through Computer Programming

To utilize a computer to solve a problem, users must give the solution in a set of instructions. Given that a program is a set of instructions necessary to solve an issue, the right statements and functionality must be included to get the desired result. For instance, if you are assigned to develop a program to add two integers (numbers), the program collects statements that accomplish the addition operation. If the program does not execute successfully, there may be an issue with your syntax. The compiler or editor will be unable to execute the program if it contains any faults or syntax errors.

Rather than memorizing lengthy methodologies or intricate procedures, programming is best learned by practice and creating codes. While it may appear to be an enjoyable hobby at first, it can quickly become time-consuming and irritating if you do not take the proper approach. Additionally, this book will assist beginners in selecting the most appropriate programming languages and easing their entry into the world of computer programming.

1.5 Advantages of Learning Coding

Many people regarded coding as an odd hobby reserved for geeks tinkering with gadgets in their basements. However, coding has transformed from a hobby to a critical employment skill over the last few years. Employers have indicated an interest in paying a premium for personnel with coding and programming skills. With that in mind, let us examine our first advantage:

Earning Profitability: One of the finest and most evident benefits of learning to code is the earning potential for coding and programming experts. The Bureau of Labor Statistics (BLS) collects and analyses pay and other employment data for a broad range of occupations.

Consider the 2019 median annual wage statistics from the Bureau of Labor Statistics for the following coding and programming-related occupations (bearing in mind the average annual wage of $45,000):

- Network and computer system administrators earn an average of $83,510.

- For web developers, the average salary is $73,760.

- Computer programmers earn an average of $86,550.

- $107,510 in compensation for software developers

- Database managers earn $93,750.

As you can see, careers that need specific programming, coding, or scripting abilities typically pay more than the national average.

A More Intelligent Perspective: It has been proven that learning to code can improve your performance in other topics that you're learning. Programming teaches you to break down big issues into separate parts and logically design a functioning program using a computer-friendly language to come up with a viable solution.

Being able to see your result in real time, you develop a unique attitude for tackling issues and dissecting data, both of which are necessary for mastering any subject. In other words, you develop the ability to view challenges from a broader perspective, adapt to the frustrations associated with reaching a roadblock and develop a plan of action to resolve them.

Coding requires critical thinking and teaches youngsters to break down complex difficulties into smaller, easier-to-manage problems. This process is known as decomposition. Even if a child does not grow up to be a software engineer or computer programmer, developing this way of thinking is transferable.

It has been said that mastering how to think is more important than mastering your thought content. Learning to code requires more than acquiring knowledge of a particular programming language. It requires cultivating an efficient and constructive approach to problem-solving that will help any new intellectual endeavor you embark on.

Job Opportunities: It appears as though there are still lots of opportunity for coding jobs.

The BLS's most recent predictions for job growth in coding and programming-related occupations are as follows:

- Web developers make around 13% of the workforce.

- 5%: Network and operating system administrators

- Computer programmers make up 7% of the workforce.

- Database administrators make about 9% of the workforce.

- 21% are application developers.

When the national average of 5% growth is considered, it is clear that a small number of jobs are growing faster than others. Computer programmers are an intriguing exception in this group, but some argue that computer programming talents are incorporated into other in-demand tech opportunities.

While the job remains incredibly valuable, a rising number of hybrid positions are being added to the workforce. As a result, fewer job advertisements for "computer programmers" are available, while more jobs incorporate programming ability into other job titles.

The technological breakthrough is pervasive in practically every aspect of life, from smart TVs and technologically enhanced kitchen equipment to online games, puzzles, and over-the-top services. Much more is occurring, and much more is predicted to come in the future years.

As a result, several new occupations are generated, and a sizable number of current jobs are redefined. This is where computer programming or coding becomes critical for people seeking the finest career opportunities or who want to better their current skills.

Coding is a game-changer, and individuals who are proficient in the language get a competitive edge in their careers. While computer programming was long considered a skill confined for computer nerds and geeks, it has gained popularity as a necessary competency and an added advantage for a wide variety of job descriptions.

It is not necessary for anyone interested in pursuing a career in computer programming to take a university course. Today, it is also an integral part of many curricula, including those in primary schools.

Coding is undoubtedly one of the most critical talents for current and future generations to acquire. For young learners, programming teaches them problem-solving abilities, growing the ability to solve an issue logically and creatively.

Additionally, coding improves one's capacity to think logically, tactically, and analytically.

Most significantly, coding is the future, making it a very valuable ability to acquire. Students that begin coding at an early age will have a plethora of progressive employment choices in the future.

Coding is a critical employment skill for today and tomorrow.

Coding is no longer a choice for young people; it is a necessary life skill. As a result, it is a terrific idea to comprehend the digital world, interact with others, be creative, and learn to code.

According to IBEF's February 2021 study on the Indian e-commerce business, the Indian e-commerce market is expected to increase from $38.5 billion in 2017 to $200 billion in 2026. With the increasing popularity and importance of e-commerce, the need for coders, software developers, and analytics specialists with coding knowledge is also increasing.

Customer expectations are also changing, as they increasingly need a simple and quick purchasing experience and personalized product recommendations. As a result, the services provided by programmers have become a critical component of retail success.

Apart from software and application developers, a variety of additional professional roles require coding proficiency. Business analysts, graphic artists, and data scientists are just a few of these job titles. Additionally, as data becomes a valuable commodity and data breaches become a growing hazard, the demand for cyber security professionals is expanding.

According to the 2021 Skills Report, software, hardware, information technology, and internet industries are predicted to hire the most people in 2021. As a result, persons with coding skills have a plenty of excellent job alternatives.

Chapter 2: What is Blockchain?

Blockchain technology represents a major change in the environment of information collecting, distribution, and governance for the world's technology users. This argument has been made often in the publications and presentations that promote and fantasize about this new future. This is one of the first books to address the topic of blockchain application development. As such, we shall outline a development strategy for developing possibilities and trends. That being stated, this is the first installment of a series tracking the progress of the Blockchain. This book is intended for developers, software engineers, and anybody else interested in the fundamentals of blockchain technology and the languages and tools necessary to create decentralized applications. We will cover everything necessary to understand the technology, writing "smart contracts," developing apps that interface with them and deploying these applications on many upcoming platforms.

Thus, let us begin. Simply described, a blockchain is a digital ledger in which transactions are recorded chronologically and publicly. A blockchain consists of a number of data blocks linked together, hence the name, with each transaction added to a new block being validated and then included. When a block is completed, it is appended to the end of the chain of blocks already in existence. Additionally, in contrast to the standard CRUD (create, read update, delete) model, the only two operations are: add transaction and view transaction. Thus, the fundamental actions of blockchain processing are as follows.

- Create new, irreversible transactions and group them into blocks.
- Verify each transaction in the block cryptographically.

- Add the new block to the end of the immutable Blockchain that already exists.

More broadly, a blockchain is also a decentralized database that stores an ordered list of multi-linked blocks. Every block is around 1 megabyte in size. It contains approximately 200 bytes of control data, such as a timestamp, a connection to a previous block, and a few other fields, as well as many transactions as possible within the remaining space.

Once recorded, the blocks are designed to be immutable; the data contained within a block cannot be modified retroactively. A public blockchain database is managed independently via a peer-to-peer system and a distributed timestamping server. Blockchains are an open, decentralized technology that enables the efficient and permanent recording of two-part transactions.

As a result, a decentralized consensus can be achieved via a public blockchain. As we will describe in further detail later, these characteristics make blockchains perfect for recording events, medical records and other types of record keeping management operations, identity management, transaction processing, and a host of other developing applications. Additionally, blockchain technologies enable large-scale and systematic collaboration on a completely decentralized basis. This can be viewed and implemented as a form of global governance, capable of controlling large-scale social interactions. For instance, in 2015, libertarian political activist Vit Jedlicka declared Gornja Siga—a seven-square-kilometre area of uninhabited forest located on the border between Croatia and Serbia—the "Free Republic of Liberland." He established a temporary government on the Bitcoin blockchain. He published a constitutional text outlining how this new country would be governed:

- Voluntary taxation
- An almost non-existent government

- No limits on speech or information

2.1 Cryptocurrency and Blockchain

When learning about cryptocurrency, one of the first terms you may encounter is "blockchain." Understanding the Blockchain is critical for understanding Bitcoin, cryptocurrency, and the promise of digital software in general. Thus, what is a blockchain, and why is it so critical?

Bitcoin is built on the Blockchain platform (or "protocol").

A distributed, peer-to-peer network controls the Blockchain.

A Blockchain is a P2P-network, which means that it is constantly saved and upgraded across multiple machines located throughout the world. Anyone can run the program to transform their computer into a "server" in this large network, contributing to the continuing transaction record. Due to the distributed concept, numerous Blockchain implementations exist worldwide, making it nearly impossible for anybody to modify transaction data once it has been registered.

It is designed to be safe:

Take Fort Knox as an example. Fort Knox is well-known as the depository for the United States' gold bullion. Fort Knox conceals a boatload of gold. Fort Knox secures this gold by employing armed guards, blast-proof vaults, and a variety of other on-site safeguards. If gold must be carried, armored trucks and troops armed with machine guns may monitor the procedure. It would be exceedingly difficult for a burglar to enter Fort Knox and steal the gold, not only because the site is heavily secured but also because gold is a tangible physical thing that would be difficult to move.

Banks (and a large number of other institutions) have historically followed a model.

When it comes to property security, a similar strategy is taken, with all items being stored nearby and protected on multiple levels. However, the great majority of financial information is now maintained as data online. We expect banks to have the cash necessary to back up the figures in our bank accounts. Yet, for the vast majority of individuals, those figures represent a value ledger rather than a physical cash balance kept in a vault at any one time.

Rather than physical vaults, we store the majority of our financial reserves electronically.

Financial data is held on a bank servers' "internet vault." Banks are attempting to transform these servers into the digital equivalents of Fort Knox. However, in today's digital transaction environment, this unified paradigm does not perform well. Whereas infiltrating Fort Knox and grabbing gold will require dynamite, specialized gear, escape vehicles, and Ocean's 11-style deception. Hackers can routinely breach bank servers and steal financial information using merely computers. Credit card fraud, identity theft, and data breaches are all genuine concerns that constantly afflict financial institutions.

Banks are continuing to add layers of encryption to their "digital" assets.

Hackers are still breaking into these "vaults." Fort Knox is ideal for storing physical gold but fails miserably when applied to digital data. Let us take a step back and examine the situation. We may begin to wonder if there is a more efficient model for storing data and handling digital transactions than attempting to secure and manage everything through a single central server. This is the application of blockchain technology.

Each block on the Blockchain is linked to the previous one.

Numerous nodes from all around the world have been openly registered. Rather than getting into a single central server and stealing or altering data, a hacker will need to alter data not only in a single block but across the entire Blockchain. Simultaneously, on the vast majority of the machines that store it worldwide.

This would technically require a significant amount of computational power.

At the moment, achieving this level of computer power would be nearly impossible. Due to the lack of centralized data storage, blockchain technology is inherently secure. If someone attempts to enter a fictitious contract, such as handing themselves non-existent Bitcoins, the Blockchain's several independent computers will discover that the sum does not add up. If the sum does not add up, the transaction is declared null and not added to the blockchain ledger.

The term "Bitcoin" is frequently used interchangeably with "Blockchain" technologies.

Smart contracts, crowdsourcing, government, intellectual property, healthcare, file management, and even the Internet of Things are just a few of the applications for this cryptocurrency. Numerous businesses are now only beginning to explore the possibilities of electronic ledgers for resource and transaction management. As a result, those interested in investing in new industries should investigate blockchain technology on its own.

This chapter discusses the problem that the Blockchain is intended to solve and why solving it is vital. This level deepens the understanding of the Blockchain's application area, the environment in which it offers the most value, and the relationship between trust, honesty, and ownership management. By the end of this section, you will have a better grasp of how the Blockchain works and a more nuanced definition of the term "Blockchain."

The Blockchain's primary objective turns out to maintain transparency in shared networks. However, why is maintaining trust so difficult in these networks, particularly tightly distributed peer-to-peer systems? We will tackle that concern by illuminating the complex relationship between the trust and honesty of tightly distributed peer-to-peer systems. As a result, you will have a deeper appreciation for the importance of honesty, as well as the honesty issue that the Blockchain can address.

The parable

Numerous languages have a graphic expression for when someone seeks to organize an unruly mob. In English, this situation is sometimes referred to as attempting to herd cats. It shows the difficulties inherent in herding a bunch of stubborn and refractory animals that refuse to recognize or consider a central authority. Is it common for you to desire to join a coalition of individuals who refuse to accept or acknowledge a central authority? This is the situation with a completely distributed peer-to-peer network composed of independent and self-contained nodes with little central control or coordination. This action exemplifies how the Blockchain addresses a significant issue in strictly distributed peer-to-peer networks.

Trust and Integrity in Peer-to-Peer Systems

The concepts of "integrity" and "trust" are synonymous. Integrity is a nonfunctional property of a software system that assures it to be secure, comprehensive, dependable, appropriate, and free of manipulation and errors. Without truth, proof, or investigation, humans have a deep belief in the honesty, legitimacy, or ability of someone or something. This is called trust. Trust is developed over time and can either increase or diminish in value based on present connections.

This means that individuals can join and contribute to a peer-to-peer community if they have faith in it. Additionally, if the consequences of their interactions with it consistently validate and deepen their trust. The integrity of the system is required to meet the needs of the users and sustain their confidence. If the system fails to re-establish users' faith due to a lack of credibility, they will abandon it, resulting in the system's demise. The major problem is establishing and maintaining credibility in a tightly distributed peer-to-peer environment, given the critical nature of confidence in peer-to-peer systems.

Credibility in tightly distributed systems is contingent on several factors, the most critical of which are as follows:

• Number of nodes or peers

• Recognized trustworthiness of peers

Knowing the number of nodes and their trustworthiness increases the odds of obtaining credibility in a distributed peer-to-peer system. This is comparable to maintaining a private club with strong moral standards and a rigorous onboarding procedure for new members. When the quantity and trustworthiness of nodes are unknown, the worst conditions for ensuring honesty in a distributed peer-to-peer system occur. This is true when an open-source, strictly distributed peer-to-peer system is running on the Internet.

Threats to the Integrity of Peer-to-Peer Systems

Two major credibility problems in peer-to-peer networks should be considered for convenience's sake:

• Errors in technology

• Peers who are malicious

Technical Inaccuracies:

Peer-to-peer networks are composed of users' computers connected over a network. The hardware and software components of a computer system and any component of a computer network all incur the risk of failing or generating problems. As a result, any distributed system must account for the risk that one or more of its components will fail or produce inaccurate results from an accident.

Peers Possess a Negative Attitude:

Malicious representatives are the second integrity threat in peer-to-peer networks. This root of untrustworthiness has nothing to do with technology. Rather, it is a problem produced by those seeking to profit from the system. This threat may be more sociological and based on group dynamics more than on technology. The most serious challenge to the peer-to-peer system comes from dishonest and manipulative peers, as they undermine the basic foundation of peer-to-peer systems, trust. Once users lose trust in their peers, they will withdraw and avoid adding processing energy to the system. As a result, membership will decline, and the scheme as a whole will become less enticing to surviving members, hastening the system's demise until it is completely abandoned.

The Mystery That Blockchain Is Supposed to Resolve:

In ideal circumstances, establishing honesty and trust is simple. In the worst-case scenario, the real issue is achieving consistency and trust in a distributed system. This is the problem that the Blockchain is intended to solve. The underlying goal of the Blockchain is to address the challenge of establishing and maintaining credibility in a strictly distributed peer-to-peer system with an undisclosed number of peers who are both untrustworthy or have no track record of trustworthiness. This is not a novel issue. Indeed, it is a well-known and widely debated topic in computer science.

Using a military metaphor, the topic is frequently referred to as the Byzantine general problem.

2.2 Bitcoin and Ethereum Blockchain

Before delving into the intricacies of Ethereum, it is critical to grasp some of the fundamental concepts behind blockchain technology in general. For those unfamiliar with the cryptocurrency industry, one of the more perplexing topics is the link between cryptocurrencies and Blockchain.

While blockchain technology is at the heart of both Bitcoin and Ethereum, both projects use the technology differently. To fully grasp how Ethereum implements the Blockchain, some familiarity with Bitcoin is beneficial.

Bitcoin was the first decentralized digital currency and the first program created on a blockchain platform. Bitcoin is by far the most popular and well-known cryptocurrency today, as well as the world's largest and most active open Blockchain. As Bitcoin gained public acceptance, several media outlets began to use "Bitcoin" and "blockchain" interchangeably. Even today, numerous articles struggle to explain the relationship between Bitcoin, other cryptocurrencies, and blockchain technology in a straightforward manner.

To ensure clarity, let us begin with the essentials. Bitcoin is, at its core, a currency. It was created to facilitate digital, secure, peer-to-peer financial transactions and has largely accomplished this purpose. Bitcoin operates based on a blockchain. On the other hand, blockchain technology has uses that reach well beyond Bitcoin and the field of digital currency in general.

Bitcoin's blockchain model works extremely well, yet there are several areas for development. (For instance, Bitcoin transactions can take a long time to process, posing a barrier of entry for many companies interested in taking Bitcoin payments.) Nobody enjoys waiting an hour in a store while a Bitcoin transaction is verified.

While Bitcoin was the first technology to deploy the Blockchain, early adopters such as Vitalik Buterin rapidly saw the Blockchain's promise in a broad range of other contexts. Because Bitcoin was created expressly to be a currency, entrepreneurs began to consider whether the Bitcoin blockchain structure was the best paradigm for developing applications other than peer-to-peer digital money transactions. Ethereum was created out of the need to provide a more flexible environment for universally leveraging the potential of blockchain technology across a diverse range of various applications.

Therefore, what is a blockchain, and how does it operate? To properly address this subject in-depth, one would have to go through some rather deep mathematical concepts, which are somewhat outside the scope of this book. Fortunately, unless you intend to become a coder, you do not need to be an expert in cryptographic hashing methods to grasp the broader concepts and structure of Blockchain.

While blockchains employ sophisticated mathematics, they are ultimately quite simple to comprehend when viewed from a bird's eye view. To begin, we have "blocks" that are connected sequentially to form a "chain." Each block contains data relating to events that occurred over a specified period. The most recent block of data offers information on recent events. In the case of Bitcoin, this data is transaction data, which includes the addresses of the Bitcoin wallets that are sending and receiving payments, the amount of currency being transacted, the time stamp of the transactions, and other similar characteristics.

Thus, each new block is a compilation of data about the most recent transactions. Each block is cryptographically secure and is linked to the previous block via a specific type of timestamp. Here, very complex arithmetic is performed to ensure that each new block corresponds to the whole history of all prior transactions on the entire Blockchain.

Each new timestamp must match the timestamp of the preceding block, which was linked to the one before that, forming a continuous chain in which each block is verifiably related to the one before it, all the way back to the very first block, dubbed the "genesis block." The whole history of every Bitcoin transaction is stored on the Blockchain, which is publicly accessible to anybody. The ability to conduct secure transactions with this level of transparency has attracted many individuals to Bitcoin and blockchain technology.

To put it simply, the Bitcoin blockchain is a record of every validated Bitcoin transaction that has ever occurred. Blocks are used to aggregate together transactions that occur over a specified period. Multiple, identical versions of the Blockchain are constantly stored and updated by a global network of participating computers. This is commonly referred to as a "distributed ledger." Fundamentally, a distributed ledger is merely a massive decentralized database or a record of data, events, or transactions. Decentralization is a fundamental principle underlying both Bitcoin and Ethereum's blockchain architectures and numerous other blockchain-based initiatives and cryptocurrencies.

Although not all distributed ledgers are blockchains, all blockchains use some form of a distributed ledger. Typically, this means that identical copies are stored and updated concurrently on many separate devices located throughout the world. In the case of Bitcoin, anyone wishing to hack or "cheat" the Blockchain would have to modify the data of not just one block but the entire historical record across the majority of the network's decentralized machines. Due to the amount of computational power necessary to accomplish this, it is almost impossible to do so under current conditions, ensuring that the system is safe by design.

Ethereum Blockchain

While not identical conceptually, the Ethereum blockchain is structured similarly. When it comes to Ethereum, the basic distinction is in the type of data stored in blocks and how that data is processed.

Today, Bitcoin remains the largest open public Blockchain and serves as the de facto blueprint for many other blockchain-based applications. The Bitcoin blockchain, on the other hand, is merely one implementation of blockchain technology. As more sectors investigate the potential of Blockchain, new models emerge regularly, frequently tailored to a particular purpose.

When we examine Bitcoin, we notice that its primary objective is to function as a decentralized, peer-to-peer digital currency. Bitcoin addresses a specific issue: how to conduct safe financial transactions peer-to-peer from anywhere globally without relying on trust, an intermediary, or a centralized authority such as a bank. While Bitcoin is not perfect, it has been fairly effective in terms of accomplishing its stated objective.

As developers and entrepreneurs recognized the potential for blockchain technology to be used for purposes other than financial transactions, many began to envision alternative blockchain architectures that would be better suited for various purposes. Vitalik Buterin, the Ethereum creator, envisioned an open platform on which anybody could create a blockchain-based application capable of performing any function.

Unlike Bitcoin's Blockchain, which is designed to store financial transaction data simply, Ethereum's Blockchain is designed to run code based on verified transactions. Rather than just transferring funds from Account A to Account B, as

Bitcoin does, Ethereum may enable a transaction from Account A to Account B to activate a wide variety of events. For instance, Ethereum transactions can be used to register a new domain name, transfer ownership of real estate, handle voter registration, and execute secure contracts between two or more parties. Hence why Ethereum "transactions" are frequently referred to as "smart contracts."

2.3 Centralized and Decentralized Systems

Due to the decentralized structure of Blockchain, it contradicts the centralized nature. This is why we are examining the debate over-centralization vs decentralization. The difference between decentralized and centralized systems is not always obvious. They are frequently misinterpreted and described inadequately. This is because there are no structures that are strictly centralized or decentralized. The majority of the concepts and examples in this part are drawn from Mr. Vitalik Buterin's notes as the creator of the Ethereum blockchain.

So, what is a distributed system exactly? Let us comprehend it first and then cross it off the list to avoid interfering with the ongoing discussion. Please keep in mind that every system, whether centralized or decentralized, can be distributed. A centralized distributed system is composed of a master node responsible for decomposing tasks or data and dispersing the burden among the nodes. On the other side, a distributed system that is decentralized does not have a "master" node, but the computing is distributed.

Let us return to our debate over-centralization vs decentralization. It is critical to keep in mind that a system's centralized/decentralized state is governed by factors other than its technological design. Meaning, a system can be centralized or decentralized in terms of technologically, but not logically or politically. Let us examine these distinct perspectives to construct a better framework that meets the demand.

Technological Architecture: A framework may be centralized or decentralized in terms of technical architecture. We consider the number of physical computers (or nodes) required to construct a system, the number of node failures that the system can withstand before failing, and so on.

Political perspective: This perspective describes the degree to which an individual, a group of individuals, or a whole organization has control over a system. If they have control over the system's computers, the system becomes centralized automatically. However, if no single individual or party dominates the system and everyone has equal access to it in a political context, the system is decentralized.

A system can be theoretically centralized or decentralized based on its appearance, regardless of functionally or politically centralized or decentralized. Another example is that if you vertically divide a system (say, computing equipment) into two halves, each with its own set of service providers and consumers, the halves are decentralized if they can function as independent units and centralized if they cannot.

Both perspectives, as mentioned earlier, are critical when designing a real-world structure and determining whether it should be centralized or decentralized. To dispel any doubts, consider the following examples that integrate these perspectives:

- Corporations are centralized architecturally (one headquarters), politically (under the leadership of a CEO or a board of directors), and conceptually. (Cutting them in half is impossible.)

- Every aspect of our contact language is decentralized — architectural, political, and logical. By and large, when two people connect, their language is neither politically affected nor logically dependent on the communication languages of other people.

- BitTorrent and comparable torrent systems are completely decentralized. Because every node can act as a provider or a buyer, the device can be halved and still function.

- On the other hand, while the Content Distribution Network is technically and architecturally decentralized, it is economically centralized because a business operates it. Amazon CloudFront is one such service.

Right now, let us have a look at Blockchain. The purpose of Blockchain technology was to enable decentralization. As a result, it is decentralized structurally. Politically, it is also decentralized, with no one in charge. Technically, it is centralized, as there is a single agreed-upon state and the entire system operates as a single global device.

Consider each of these terms independently and in comparison to understanding why Blockchain is supposed to be decentralized.

Centralized Systems:

As the name implies, a unified system is one in which all administrative functions are coordinated through a single management point. While such systems are straightforward to establish, administer, enforce, and rule, they have various inherent flaws, including the following:

- They are less robust because they include a single point of failure.

- They are more prone to attack and thus less secure.

- Concentrating power can result in immoral behavior.

- Scalability is frequently a problem.

Decentralized Systems:

As the name implies, a decentralized structure lacks centralized power and grants equal authority to each node. Building, managing, controlling, and enforcing confidence in such systems is not easy. They do not, however, have the drawbacks associated with typical centralized structures. Several advantages of decentralized systems include the following:

- They do not have a single point of failure, making them more reliable and less prone to failure.

- It is more stable due to the lack of a concentrated point of attack.

- Symmetrical authority structure that limits the scope of immoral activity and is often democratic

2.4 Smart Contracts

The term "Smart Contracts" is frequently used in conjunction with Ethereum. What is the definition of a smart contract? In a nutshell, a smart contract is a computer program. Smart contracts are the "meat and potatoes" of Ethereum, and it is worth delving deeper into this notion to appreciate the platform's strength and vision fully.

Do not be concerned if you lack a strong technical background. When writing smart contracts, you will either need to learn to code or hire a programmer, but you do not need to know how to code to grasp how smart contracts function theoretically. However, having a fundamental understanding of how computer program functions is beneficial, even if you do not know how to build them yourself.

While computer programs are capable of incredible complexity, they all operate by asking a sequence of yes or no questions. When we consider that all "data" is ultimately made up of 1's and 0's, or binary code, the 1's and 0's represent "yes's" and "no's." In general, a computer has no "maybes."

When we consider digital transactions involving Bitcoin, what we are doing is executing a basic computer program. What occurs is that Person A sends monies to Person B. Bitcoin's program will prompt you with the following questions: Is Person A truly self-sufficient? Is it possible for Person A to verify ownership of the address where those assets are being held? Is Person B's address valid? As long as the necessary inputs are provided, the decentralized Bitcoin network will establish a consensus to do the computations and execute the program: the transaction will be verified, and Person B will receive the monies.

With Bitcoin, the running software is limited to one sort of transaction. "Bitcoins" are simply just numbers transferred from one digital address to another, and the Blockchain keeps track of all of these transactions. The Blockchain is a distributed ledger technology that enables a decentralized network of computers to establish consensus on which tasks to perform and then accomplish those activities. While "duties" in the instance of Bitcoin are transactions between Person A and Person B, is there any reason why this system could not be utilized to manage other types of tasks? No, and it is precisely what Ethereum is designed to accomplish. Ethereum is executed on top of the same blockchain technology as Bitcoin, but it enables the execution of any program.

Even if we continue to conceive financial transactions, Ethereum's capabilities provide for things like conditions, resulting in a much more flexible environment for payment systems. For instance, with Ethereum, a secure deposit might be stored on the Blockchain for a specific amount of time and returned to the payer if certain requirements were not met; if the circumstances were met, the payment might be released to the payee. Without the involvement of a third party, there is no way to store a payment in "escrow" in this manner in Bitcoin. This is a simple example of a conditional transaction that might be executed via a smart contract in Ethereum.

Smart contracts bring up a new universe of possibilities as we become more integrated with the Internet of Things. For instance, if smart cars become more widespread, we can readily foresee a transition away from the traditional paying for parking via a parking meter and toward a system solely based on smart contracts. Sensors could easily be used to associate certain vehicles with specific parking spaces. A smart contract could be used to deduct the appropriate price based on the amount of time a vehicle was parked in a given location. Rather than searching for change beneath the seat or negotiating parking meters, vehicles could park, and the smart contract would do the transaction in the background. Cities might eliminate the need for meter maids and automate the entire process.

Despite their basic differences, many people regard Bitcoin and Ethereum as "competitors" vying for control of the blockchain space. This perspective is not entirely accurate even for individuals who are only concerned with Ether as money and have no interest in technology. Bitcoin and Ethereum are two independent, coexisting technologies with distinct objectives and purposes. Bitcoin is intended to function as a medium of exchange; it is not a means to an end. Ethereum makes use of Ether to facilitate the execution of smart contracts; the Ether currency serves as a means to an end. In this way, the two projects are complementary, as they have distinct visions, objectives, and uses.

To better understand smart contracts and how the Ethereum platform works, it is helpful to review certain software development fundamentals. If you have executed any programming language, you will have an advantage in understanding how smart contracts execute code. If not, have no fear. Again, you do not need to write code to grasp how Ethereum works, although it is beneficial to familiarize yourself with some fundamental programming ideas.

Chapter 3: IDE and Frameworks

An integrated development environment (IDE) is a type of software that merges commonly used development tools into a unified graphical user interface (GUI) to develop applications Typically, an IDE comprises of the following:

Source Code: A source code editor is a text editor that aids in the development of software code by emphasizing syntax with visual cues, giving language-specific auto-completion, and automatically checking for defects as code is produced.

Local build automation: Tools that automate routine operations associated with making a local build of software for developer use, such as packaging binary code, compiling source code into binary code, and performing automated tests

Debugger: A program used to test other programs that visually display a defect's location in the source code.

3.1 The Main Concept of IDEs

An IDE helps developers quickly create new apps since many tools are not required to be integrated manually during the setup phase. Additionally, developers save time by not spending hours on learning how to utilize many different tools when they are all represented on the same workbench. This is particularly advantageous for onboarding new engineers, who may rely on an IDE to quickly become familiar with a team's standard tools and procedures. Indeed, most features in integrated development environments (IDEs) are designed to save time, such as intelligent code completion and automatic code generation, which eliminates the need to write out whole character sequences.

Other popular IDE features are intended to assist developers in organizing their work and resolving issues. IDEs parse code as it is written, allows for real-time detection of problems caused by human mistakes. Since a single graphical user interface presents utilities, developers may perform operations without moving between apps.

Syntax highlighting is also a feature included in most integrated development environments (IDEs), which employs visual signals to distinguish between different types of grammar in the text editor. Additionally, several IDEs feature class, object explorers and representations of the class hierarchy for certain languages.

It is possible to develop apps without using an IDE or for each developer to create their IDE manually. The advantage of this method for certain developers is the extreme customizability and control it provides. However, in a corporate setting, the time savings, environment consistency, and automation capabilities of current IDEs typically surpass any other benefits.

Before the advent of integrated development environments, programmers created their scripts in text editors. This entailed composing and saving a program in a text editor before running it through the compiler, noting any error warnings, and then returning to the text editor to update their code.

It was not until 1983 that Borland Ltd. bought a Pascal compiler and released it as TurboPascal, the first language to provide an integrated editor and compiler

While TurboPascal popularized the concept of an integrated development environment, many feel Microsoft's Visual Basic (VB), released in 1991 to be the first true IDE. Visual Basic was a widely-used programming language throughout the 1980s. It was written in the earlier BASIC language. With the advent of Visual Basic, programming could be conceived of in graphical terms, resulting in significant productivity gains.

Today, most enterprise development teams choose a pre-configured integrated development environment (IDE) optimized for their unique use case; hence, the decision is not whether to implement an IDE but which IDE to choose.

3.2 The Advantages of IDEs

Integrated development environments help developers to be more productive. These IDEs increase productivity by reducing setup time, increasing the pace of development activities, keeping developers informed of the newest best practices and security concerns, and streamlining the development process to ensure that everyone is on the same page.

Faster setup: Without an IDE interface, programmers must spend time setting different development tools. By incorporating an IDE, programmers can access the same set of capabilities in one location, eliminating the need to switch tools frequently.

Faster development tasks: Improved developer productivity is a result of deeper integration of development tasks. For instance, developers may scan code and validate syntax as they edit, providing rapid feedback when syntax problems are made. Programmers are no longer need to move between applications to complete tasks. Additionally, the IDE's tools and features assist programmers in organizing resources, avoiding errors, and implementing shortcuts.

Additionally, IDEs can aid in reorganizing the development process by supporting holistic planning. They encourage programmers to consider their activities in the context of the complete development lifecycle (SDLC) rather than as a collection of discrete jobs.

Learning: Another advantage is the opportunity to keep updated and educated. For instance, an IDE's help topics are continually updated with new samples, project templates, and enhancements. Continuously learning and staying updated on the best practices enables developers to bring value to their team and organization, increasing productivity.

Standardization: Standardization also governs the development process, allowing programmers to collaborate effortlessly and enabling recruits to ramp up to speed quickly.

3.3 Commonly Used IDEs

There are several technical and business applications for IDEs, implying numerous proprietary and open-source IDE solutions. Typically, the essential aspects that distinguish IDEs are as follows:

The range of supported languages: Some IDEs are language-specific and better suited to a particular programming style. For example, IntelliJ is largely recognized as a Java integrated development environment (IDE). Other IDEs, such as the Eclipse IDE, support various languages in one package, including Java, XML, and Python.

Supported operating system(s): A developer's operating system will narrow down which IDEs are feasible (unless the IDE is cloud-based) and if the application created is meant for an end-user running a certain operating system (such as Android or iOS), this constraint may be amplified.

While most IDEs have the three critical capabilities of a text editor, build automation, and debugger, many also incorporate refactoring, code search, and continuous integration and deployment (CI/CD) tools.

Impact on system performance: If a developer wishes to run other memory-intensive apps concurrently, the memory footprint of an IDE may be critical to consider.

Extensions and plugins: Some IDEs enable developers to tailor processes to their specific requirements and preferences.

Integrated development environments for mobile devices

Almost every sector has been impacted by the growing popularity of smartphone and tablet applications, which has prompted many businesses to build mobile applications in addition to traditional web applications. Platform selection is a critical component in mobile application development. For example, if a new application will be used on iOS, Android, and a web page, it may be prudent to begin with an IDE that supports several operating systems.

Cloud-based integrated development environments

Unlike local development environments, IDEs delivered as a cloud-based Software-as-a-Service (SaaS) provide several distinct advantages. For starters, as is the case with any SaaS product, there is no need to download software or establish local environments and dependencies, which enables developers to begin contributing to projects instantly. Additionally, this gives a level of homogeneity across team members' environment, which can help minimize the frequently encountered "this works on my machine, why does not it work on yours" issue. Additionally, because the development environment is centrally maintained, no code is stored on the computer of an individual developer, which alleviates worries about intellectual property and security.

Processes also have a varied effect on local computers. Because processes like building and testing are often compute-intensive, developers are unlikely to continue using their workstations while a process is ongoing. A cloud-based integrated development environment (IDE) can dispatch long-running processes without monopolizing the computational resources of a local workstation. Additionally, cloud IDEs are often platform-agnostic, allowing for access to a variety of cloud suppliers.

Developers must choose an IDE that is appropriate for the sort of application they intend to create. For instance, if a developer wants to create an iOS application, an IDE that accepts Apple's Swift programming language is required. IDEs come in various forms from web- and cloud-based to mobile, language-specific, and multi-language.

Web-based integrated development environments (IDEs) are ideal for developing web-based applications in HTML, JavaScript, or comparable programming languages. Microsoft's Visual Studio Code is a web-based integrated development environment (IDE) that includes syntax highlighting, a code editor, code completion, and debugging.

IDEs are increasingly being delivered via a platform as a service (PaaS) architecture. The advantages of these cloud-based integrated development environments (IDEs) include remote access to software development tools from any suitable device, little to no download and installation requirements, and ease of cooperation among geographically dispersed developers. Cloud9 is an AWS-hosted integrated development environment (IDE) that supports up to 40 languages, including C, C++, Python, Ruby, and JavaScript. Cloud9 provides users with code completion, an image editor, and a debugger and additional capabilities such as support for Microsoft Azure and Heroku deployments (which is a cloud-based PaaS IDE).

Typically, an integrated development environment (IDE) for mobile development works with code that runs on android or IOS devices. Xamarin is an example of a cross-platform mobile integrated development environment (IDE), which implies that it can generate code for various mobile platform types. For instance, a developer may create a feature in C, and Xamarin will automatically convert it to Swift for iOS and Java for Android. Additionally, Xamarin provides user interface testing and the ability to deploy beta tests to consumers.

Language-specific integrated development environments (IDEs) such as C-Free — including a code editor, debugger, and an environment for running C and C++ programs — are available. Other IDEs, such as the previously mentioned Cloud9 and Visual Studio Code, allow numerous languages. Among the most popular IDEs are NetBeans, Eclipse, and IntelliJ IDEA.

Disambiguation: IDE may also refer to integrated drive electronics.

3.4 Blockchain Development Tools

Blockchain is the market's fastest-growing skill set today. Due to the enormous success of Bitcoin, every business now wants a piece of the action (it is Blockchain!). After all, blockchain technology is an exciting field with enormous potential for advancement. This has increased demand for qualified Blockchain specialists, now the market's most highly compensated professionals. However, finding work in Blockchain is not easy. First, you must have the necessary skills and, most crucially, the ability to deal with the various blockchain tools required for blockchain development.

A Blockchain education from a reputable university will significantly increase your chances of finding a job at large corporations. Additionally, if you intend to remain relevant in the market and provide your services to a reputable firm, you must maximize the potential of Blockchain development tools.

Blockchain tools not only streamline the blockchain development process but also assist you in improving your topic expertise.

Solidity

Without question, Solidity is one of the most popular programming languages utilized by blockchain engineers.

It was created keeping C++, Python, and JavaScript in mind and is optimized for the Ethereum Virtual Machine. Solidity is dynamically typed and includes inheritance, libraries, and sophisticated user-defined types.

Solidity adheres to the OOP paradigm and is most frequently used for the development of smart contracts. Solidity enables blockchain developers to create apps that execute self-enforcing business logic in smart contracts, resulting in a non-repudiable and authentic record of transactions. This is useful for constructing voting contracts, crowdfunding campaigns, multi-signature wallets, and blind auctions.

Follow this link to visit their website and learn more:

https://soliditylang.org/

Geth

Geth is a Go-based implementation of an Ethereum node. It comes with three interfaces: a JSON-RPC server, a command-line interface, and an interactive console. Geth is compatible with all three major operating systems i.e., Windows, Mac, and Linux and can construct blockchain applications.

Geth is used for various functions on the Ethereum Blockchain, including token contracts, ether mining, smart contract creation, and block history exploration. Once Geth is installed, you may connect to an existing blockchain or construct your own. The good news is that Geth simplifies matters by connecting immediately to the Ethereum main net.

Follow this link to visit their website and learn more:

https://geth.ethereum.org/

Blockchain Testnet

Blockchain Testnet is the last addition to the list of the top blockchain tools accessible right now.It is a fundamental tool for blockchain developers and is useful for pre-production testing of decentralized applications. Each blockchain solution has its own Blockchain Testnet, optimized for best performance with the respective blockchain solution.

When it comes to Blockchain development, the value of the Blockchain Testnet cannot be overstated. A Blockchain Testnet enables you to evaluate decentralized applications (dApps) before launching them live. Each blockchain solution has its Testnet, and it is strongly advised that you utilize the Testnet associated with that solution for the best results. There are three different types of Blockchain Testnets: public, private, and GanacheCLI. Testnets are incredibly beneficial since they enable you to test your decentralized applications thoroughly for faults and problems without investing a lot of money or resources. For instance, Ethereum utilizes gas as a fuel source for several functions. Spending money on petrol each time you need to perform a test drive can quickly add up to a significant financial burden.

Testing becomes possible as a result of Testnets. Users may choose from three distinct types of Blockchain Testnets: public, private, and Ganache CLI. Testnet is a useful resource for identifying flaws and vulnerabilities in decentralized applications without requiring large financial inputs. Gorli Testnet is now one of the most popular among developers.

Follow this link to visit their website and learn more:

https://www.blockchain.com/explorer?view=btc-testnet

Ganache

As a Truffle Suite Blockchain tool, Ganache enables Blockchain developers to establish their own private Ethereum blockchain for testing decentralized applications, analyzing state, and executing commands while maintaining complete control over the chain's operation.

Ganache is a Truffle Suite Blockchain tool that enables you to construct your own private Ethereum blockchain for testing decentralized applications, executing commands, and inspecting state while maintaining complete control over the chain's operation.

The most significant feature of Ganache is that it enables users to do any operations that are possible on the main chain without paying for them. Ganache is a widely popular Blockchain tool among developers due to its features, including an integrated block explorer and powerful mining controls. Blockchain engineers use Ganache to test their smart contracts throughout the development process.

Follow this link to visit their website and learn more:

Embark

As a developer platform for Ethereum decentralized applications, Embark enables developers to create and deploy decentralized applications quickly. Additionally, it enables users to design and deploy serverless HTML5 applications that take an application of decentralized technology. Additionally, one can use Embark to develop smart contracts and make them accessible in the JS code. If the contract is amended, Embark and the associated Dapp will adjust it independently.

In the case of numerous contracts, migration, redeployment, and modifications are all readily handled. To interface with Embark, one may utilize a regular web development language and any build workflow. Embark enables developers to write contracts using Javascript on a test-driven basis and manage their contracts across many blockchains.

Follow this link to visit their website and learn more:

https://framework.embarklabs.io/

Truffle

Truffle is a significant rival among the top blockchain tools. It is an Ethereum blockchain framework designed to simplify the development of Ethereum-based applications by providing a development environment. Additionally, Truffle contains a vast library of custom deployments that enable the creation of new smart contracts and the resolution of blockchain development difficulties.

Additionally, Truffle is well-suited for developing complicated Ethereum decentralized applications. Automated contract testing is another major feature of Truffle as a blockchain tool. Truffle can automate contract testing using Mocha and Chai. Additionally, Truffle can assist in facilitating the development of smart contracts and their linkage, compilation, and deployment. Notably, Truffle also has a customizable build pipeline that enables the execution of bespoke build methods.

Follow this link to visit their website and learn more:

https://trufflesuite.com/

Metamask

At the moment, the majority of blockchain technology usage is focused on cryptocurrencies. Thus, wallets are also considered the greatest blockchain tools, while Metamask offers some additional features. It acts as a bridge between a web browser and the Ethereum blockchain.

Additionally, Metamask provides a software platform for providing Ether and other ERC-20-compliant assets. Simultaneously, it enables interaction with Ethereum's decentralized applications. The browser-based capability may contribute to Metamask's simplicity of usage. It is critical to understand that users may connect Coinbase and Shapeshift to Metamask to sell and acquire ERC20 tokens and ETH.

Additionally, users may utilize Metamask to store keys for ETH and ERC20 tokens. Metamask is compatible with various Ethereum test networks, making it an ideal wallet for blockchain engineers. After installing the app in the browser, users will have access to an integrated Ethereum wallet.

Follow this link to visit their website and learn more:

https://metamask.io/

Parity

Parity is an Ethereum client. This is another powerful platform among blockchain engineers since it is a mission-critical management tool. Additionally, parity makes use of the Rust programming language. Another fantastic aspect of this technology is that it gives an infrastructure that is both fast and dependable.

In any case, creating your blockchain network for personal or commercial use, or even simply for research purposes, is simple. To put it another way, all of these are fully customizable.

Follow this link to visit their website and learn more:

https://www.parity.io/technologies/ethereum/

3.5 Blockchain Development Frameworks

As with a peer-to-peer network, blockchain technology is built on decentralized networking technologies. The decentralization of the Blockchain is similar to that of Napster: each party in the network is linked to the others. This is not your typical client-server network. Each node in a blockchain network performs both client and server functions.

In a blockchain network, nodes maintain and share a public database, ledger, or record. This ledger contains transactions of network transactions, which are confirmed by majority consensus on the network. Once a new transaction has been confirmed and recorded in the ledger, the ledger is broadcast to all network nodes. Thus, the nodes have access to the current ledger, which contains the most recent transactions.

It is simple to see why businesses across several industries use blockchain technology to enable safe transactions of valuable assets such as digital information, real estate, and cash.

Without further ado, let us look at six of the most popular frameworks for building blockchain-based applications. We will highlight essential features and break down strengths and shortcomings to assist you in making an educated decision when developing your blockchain network on the proper platform.

Ethereum

Ethereum is the world's most frequently used and popular blockchain development platform. Indeed, it is the development's first platform for developing blockchain applications. Built-in 2015, it pioneered a new concept known as the smart contract.

A smart contract is a computer program comprised of functions and states. Each smart contract on the Ethereum blockchain is paired with a unique address. Because smart contracts are an independent sort of account on Ethereum, they can send transactions and maintain a balance.

The Ethereum Virtual Machine is another incredible aspect of Ethereum (EVM). In EVM, a virtual machine is a computer that runs Ethereum accounts and smart contracts.

The EVM supports the development of Ethereum-based decentralized applications (DApps). The variety of DApp use cases is rapidly extending beyond banking into industries as diverse as healthcare, logistics, real estate, and the legal system, to name a few.

Ethereum's smart contracts are implemented using the Solidity programming language. Etheruem is a permission less ledger that is available to the public. Its consensus process is known to be rather slow: proof of work.

Ethereum has its coin, Ether. On the Ethereum blockchain, Ether is used to pay for the creation and initialization of transactions.

Hyper ledger Fabric

The Hyperledger Hub created Hyperledger Fabric, a permissioned distributed ledger platform. The Hyperledger Hub is a Linux Foundation initiative that fosters the open development of centralized and decentralized blockchain systems.

Fabric is geared for businesses looking to use, integrate, or build blockchain-based solutions and applications.

Not only is Hyperledger Fabric comparable to Ethereum in terms of permissions ledger technology, but also terms of its modular design. Fabric's flexibility enables a plug-and-play interface for users to choose their desired services, such as the consensus method and smart contract types.

Additionally, Hyperledger Fabric enables smart contracts. On Fabric, smart contracts may be written in Go, Java, or JavaScript.

Hyperledger Sawtooth

Hyperledger Sawtooth is another modular blockchain technology developed by the Hyperledger Hub to build distributed ledger applications and networks. The Linux Foundation released Hyperledger Sawtooth, which IBM and Digital Assets presently support.

Enterprises leverage Hyperledger Sawtooth to develop scalable and resilient systems and implement highly secure blockchain solutions. Hyperledger Sawtooth, like Fabric and Ethereum, is a permissioned ledger.

Hyperledger Sawtooth is equipped with several advanced features and integrations, including the following:

Seth (Sawtooth-Ethereum) connection, which enables the deployment of Etheruem smart contracts on Hyperledger Sawtooth, Parallel processing, which enables quicker transaction processing than other blockchain systems,

A dynamic, undefined consensus protocol means that the consensus method can be changed at any moment.

In terms of consensus algorithms, Hyperledger Sawtooth supports a variety of them, including the following:

The PoET (proof of elapsed time) technique leverages secure instruction execution to deliver the scalability benefits of a Nakamoto-style consensus process without the power consumption disadvantages associated with proof of work algorithms.

PBFT (practical Byzantine fault tolerance), a voting-based algorithm that votes for agreement among network participants by utilizing dynamic network membership, regular view modifications, and block catch-up procedure characteristics.

Raft is a consensus engine that is based on and leverages Raft. The logs of reasonably independent subproblems are used to agree on a value and reach a judgment in this consensus.

EOSIO

EOSIO is a high-performance, open-source blockchain platform that Block. one introduced in 2018. EOSIO is a platform for developing blockchain apps which is quick, dependable, and extremely secure.

EOSIO enables the deployment of smart contracts on its established networks. Additionally, you may create your EOSIO networks and use them to implement smart contracts.

EOSIO smart contracts are written in C++. The official documentation on how to develop and deploy smart contracts using EOSIO can be found here.

Though not as well-known as Ethereum or Bitcoin, EOSIO offers some distinct selling qualities. Developers prefer EOSIO for their blockchain applications because it is:

- Rapid and effective.

- Configurable to a fault

- Extremely secure

- Extremely compatible

- Developer-focused

As a bonus, the EOSIO website does an excellent job of keeping the community informed of current events and news.

Corda

Corda is an open-source blockchain platform developed in 2015 by the R3 Consortium. Corda was originally intended for financial institutions but has subsequently been expanded to include healthcare, insurance, digital assets, and finance. The next-generation blockchain architecture promotes itself as "the preferred distributed ledger technology platform for financial services and beyond."

Corda is a permissioned ledger that supports smart contracts, which means that smart contracts may be written and deployed on the Corda blockchain.

Smart contracts in Corda may be written in either Java or Kotlin.

Because the platform lacks a mining component, a portion of the transactions are never seen in most nodes. Corda transactions, in other words, are not available to all nodes. Corda does not support cryptocurrencies or tokens.

Corda is a pluggable consensus protocol, which implies that it supports a large number of consensus techniques.

Corda possesses validity, consensus, and uniqueness in consensus. Validity consensus verifies that all state contracts approve the transaction and contain all needed signatures.

If the transaction inputs are unique and have not been utilized in previous transactions, unique consensus agrees on a value.

Quorum

Quorum is an open-source Ethereum-based blockchain platform. It was launched in 2016 to serve the banking industry and enable businesses to "use Ethereum for their high-value blockchain applications."

ConsenSys just bought Quorum from JP Morgan. Numerous firms, including Microsft, JP Morgan, Covantis, the South African Reserve Bank, SiaChain, and Komgo, trust Quorum and have used it in their operations.

Quorum assists businesses interested in using the blockchain platform. It utilizes a permissioned ledger but also allows for client-specific customization. Additionally, Quorum facilitates the creation of public and private networks, as well as smart contracts.

As with Ethereum, smart contracts in Quorum are written in Solidity, which simplifies migrating from Ethereum to Quorum. Quorum's consensus process is based on voting; it agrees to a transaction and a block-based on their votes from nodes.

Although there are other blockchain development frameworks available, the ones listed here are the most widely used.

Chapter 4: How to Become a Blockchain Developer

This step of learning is the book's cornerstone since it teaches how the blockchain operates inside. This stage's learning activities will take you through all of the blockchain's principles and underlying technology. By the end of this level, you will have a firm grasp of all of the blockchain's fundamental principles, how they operate independently, and how they work together to form the massive apparatus known as the blockchain.

4.1 Planning the Blockchain

The fundamental ideas behind the blockchain-based system for maintaining ownership:

Blockchain Design

The preceding phases established a connection between trust, integrity, and completely distributed peer-to-peer networks, as well as the blockchain. Consequently, you now have a firm grasp of what blockchain technology is, why it is necessary, and what problem it resolves. However, you remain unaware of the core workings of the blockchain. Additionally, it covers the primary responsibilities involved in developing a blockchain for ownership management and gives an overview of the key principles.

Objective

The purpose of this section is to familiarize yourself with blockchain principles. I will offer the task of creating your ownership management system for educational purposes.

Thus, you will face the same issues that the blockchain's inventor did: creating software that handles ownership in a truly distributed peer-to-peer system of ledgers that functions in an entirely open and untrustworthy environment.

Commencement

To begin, the following summarizes the key facts concerning the system under consideration:

- The system will be entirely distributed peer-to-peer, relying on system-contributed computational resources.

- The peer-to-peer system connects the individual nodes over the Internet.

- The number of nodes, as well as their trustworthiness and dependability, are unknown.

- The peer-to-peer system's objective is to manage the ownership of a digital good (e.g., sales bonus points or digital money).

The Way to Proceed

Seven primary issues must be solved when building and implementing a software system for managing ownership in an open and untrustworthy environment through the use of a purely distributed peer-to-peer ledger system:

- Descriptors of ownership

- Ownership protection

- Keeping track of transactions

- Preparation of ledgers for distribution in an insecure environment

- Distribute ledgers

- Updating ledgers with fresh transactions

- Determining which ledgers contain the truth

1st Task: Defining ownership

Before you can begin constructing the blockchain, you must determine its purpose. You will be developing a software system to handle ownership, so you must first decide how to define ownership. Transactions, it turns out, are an excellent method to represent any transfer of ownership, and the whole history of transactions is critical for identifying the current owners.

2nd Task: Protecting ownership

Using transactions to define ownership is only the beginning. Additionally, you must have a method for preventing unauthorized access to other people's property. In reality, you can prevent anyone from using your automobile or entering your house by installing locks on your doors. Cryptography provides a mechanism for protecting transactions on an individual level, analogous to how locks on doors safeguard your particular automobile or house.

Protecting ownership entails three primary components: identifying and authenticating owners and limiting owners' access to the property. These procedures will also provide fascinating insights for anyone with a technical background or familiarity with hash values.

3rd Task: Transaction Data Storage

Defining ownership in transactions and implementing security mechanisms that protect ownership at the transaction level are critical stages in developing a software system that controls ownership. However, you will require a method to store the whole history of transactions, as this will be utilized to establish ownership. Because the transaction history is secure for establishing ownership, it must be securely preserved. The blockchain-data structure is the digital counterpart of a ledger.

4th Task: Preparation of Ledgers for Distribution in an Untrustworthy Environment

While having a single isolated ledger or blockchain data structure containing transaction data is advantageous, the goal is to create a distributed peer-to-peer system of ledgers that functions in an untrustworthy environment. As a result, you will have copies of the ledger operating on unreliable nodes in an unreliable network. Additionally, you will delegate control of the ledgers to the whole network, eliminating the need for a single point of control or coordination. How do you guard against faked or modified ledgers e.g., by removing or adding unlawful transactions to history? As it turns out, the most effective strategy to prevent transaction histories from being altered is to make them immutable. This implies that once ledgers and later transaction histories are created, they cannot be modified.

As a consequence, you will never have to worry about the ledgers being altered or falsified, as they cannot be altered in the first place. However, having a distributed peer-to-peer system with unchangeable ledgers seems extremely secure but ultimately pointless, as it will prevent you from adding new transactions. Thus, the blockchain-data-problem structure is to remain immutable on the one hand while still admitting new transactions on the other. As a result, the blockchain data structure is append-only. New transactions may be added, but it is not easy to modify previously contributed data.

5th Task: Distribute the Ledgers

Once the ledger is append-only, it is possible to establish a distributed peer-to-peer ledger system by making copies available to anybody who requests them. However, just supplying copies of append-only ledgers will not accomplish your objectives. A distributed system that controls ownership requires communication between peers or nodes.

6th Task: Updating the Ledgers with New Transactions

The distributed peer-to-peer system members will retain individual copies of an append-only blockchain data structure on their computers. Because the data structure supports additional transaction data, you must guarantee that only genuine and permitted transactions are added. This is accomplished by allowing all members of the peer-to-peer system to add new data and transform each member of the peer-to-peer system into a peer supervisor. As a consequence, all members will oversee one another and point attention to their peers' errors.

7th Task: Determining Which Ledgers Accurately Reflect the Truth

Once new transactions may be added to the peer-to-peer system's ledgers, an issue occurs that is characteristic of any distributed peer-to-peer system: different peers may have received different transactions, and their history of transactions soon diverges. As a result, in a peer-to-peer system, many copies of the transaction history may exist. Given that the transaction history serves as the foundation for identifying authorized owners, having contradictory transaction histories poses a severe danger to the system's integrity. Thus, it is critical to discover a technique to either prevent the creation of several transaction histories or determine which transaction history reflects the truth. The previous technique is not practicable due to the nature of a purely distributed peer-to-peer system.As a result, you require a criterion for determining and selecting the single transaction history that accurately represents the truth. However, there is another issue: in a truly distributed peer-to-peer system, no central authority can determine which transaction history must be picked.

It turns out that one may resolve this issue by requiring each node in the peer-to-peer system to independently choose which transaction history reflects the truth in a fashion that the majority of peers agree on. Additionally, it turns out that the way the blockchain allows for the addition of new transactions to the append-only blockchain data structure already has the answer to this problem.

Outlook

This stage defines seven challenges that give a strenuous intellectual journey via the blockchain's principles. Once these challenges are completed, you will reach the summit: a comprehension of the blockchain.

To create a purely distributed peer-to-peer system of ledgers for managing ownership, the following challenges must be addressed:

- Determining ownership
- Protecting ownership from illegal access
- Storing transaction data
- Preparing ledgers for distribution in an untrustworthy environment
- Forming a system of distributed ledgers
- Adding and confirming new transactions to the ledgers

4.2 Using The Blockchain

We have already discussed what a blockchain is, its use, and how it operates. However, the blockchain was not invented, so that we might waste time debating its technical concepts. Rather than that, the blockchain was invented for real-world applications. As a result, this stage delves deeper into the application of the blockchain. Additionally, it specifies generic blockchain application patterns and connects them to the blockchain's features. Additionally, this stage sketches some blockchain applications and discusses the details that should be addressed while examining a particular blockchain application.

The Allegory

Why are shelves, cabinets, drawers, and boxes used? These storage methods are frequently utilized since they allow for the storing and organization of items regardless of their intended function. A box can be used to hold a variety of items, including documents, technical spare parts, office supplies, photographs, money, DVDs, clothing, and wine bottles. The versatility of boxes, drawers, cabinets, and shelves is limited only by the diversity of goods stored in them. However, I will first discuss the blockchain's capabilities as a specific box for digital objects.

The Blockchain's Characteristics

The blockchain is a decentralized peer-to-peer data storage system that possesses the following properties:

- Immutable
- Append-only
- Ordered
- Time-stamped
- Transparent and open

- Secure (identification, authentication, and authorization)

These qualities of the blockchain are agnostic to the data that is stored on it. Thus, the blockchain may be thought of as a specific type of box for keeping digital goods from a basic point. This paves the way for a plethora of blockchain-based applications.

Patterns of Generic Application

We can come up with the following generic use cases based on the blockchain's features and its attribute of being a generic data repository for all types of data:

- Proof of existence

- Proof of non-existence

- Proof of time

- Proof of order

- Proof of identity

- Proof of authorship

- Proof of ownership

Proof of Existence

This application of the blockchain is focused on storing data solely to prove its existence. As a result, this application does not make use of the blockchain's ordering or time-stamping capabilities. For example, registries of goods that supposed to be unique, such as brand names, patents, license codes, and Internet or e-mail addresses, are concrete applications.

Proof Non-existence

This application of the blockchain is the polar opposite of proof of existence.

It enables the verification of whether particular entries or items do not exist on the blockchain. Complaints, penalties, or convictions are all examples of concrete applications of this.

Proof of time

The existence of an entry in the blockchain is significant in this scenario and the moment at which the record was added. The blockchain may fulfil this requirement since the blocks of the blockchain data structure retain the time stamp of when adding them began. The blockchain's time-stamped features enable applications that track the occurrence of events across time, such as tracking delivery or notice, tracking payments, tracking the orderly opening and closing of public bidding procedures, and managing predictions.

Proof of Order

This type of usage makes use of the blockchain's ordering feature. The blockchain's relative ordering attribute is advantageous for applications that maintain the relative ordering of events regardless of their exact time, such as tracking application processes, auditing public bidding procedures, and escrow services. Proving that a particular occurrence was the first or last is a special instance of proof of order. This type of proof is critical when resources are allocated in the same order as claims or documents are presented, such as college or university applications, patent applications, or copyright claims.

Proof of Identity

Proof of identity can be regarded as a subset of proof of existence because it establishes the existence of a particular identity. The blockchain is well-suited for this use case since it holds data that may be used to identify someone or something and implements fundamental security concepts for identification and authentication.

This usage pattern has concrete applications in the form of digital identity documents for people, animals, and objects. Governments might use blockchains to manage personal documents such as driver's licenses or passports as part of their e-government plan.

Proof of Authorship

This usage pattern focuses on proving who or what added certain data to the blockchain. The blockchain is capable of serving this role since it maintains data that is uniquely identifiable by its cryptographic fingerprint and provides fundamental security principles such as identification, authentication, and authorization. Identification and authentication are required to identify and verify writers. Authorization is required in this use case to prevent unauthorized data from being added to the blockchain. This pattern is used in various applications, including electronic publishing, tracking content changes in documents, content delivery, collaborative editing, and copyright protection.

Proof of Ownership

This usage pattern is geared toward managing and establishing ownership. It is based on all of the preceding patterns, including proof of existence, proof of order, proof of identity, and proof of authorship, as well as the three fundamental security principles of identification, authentication, and authorization. Examples of applications that use this pattern include systems for managing real estate ownership, automobiles, business stock, bonds, digital money, and cryptographic currencies.

Particular Use Cases

The blockchain is data-agnostic. As a result, the variety of data saved in the blockchain and application fields are as varied as human activities themselves.

As a result, providing a comprehensive overview of all blockchain applications is impractical. As a result, this section highlights a few real blockchain application areas where the blockchain is either being utilized or will be employed in the near future1:

- **Payments:** Managing digital fiat currency ownership and transfer.

- **Cryptocurrencies:** Managing the ownership and generation of digital payment instruments not backed by any government, central bank, or other central organization.

- **Micropayments:** The transmission of little sums of money that would be too expensive to send via standard forms of payment.

- **Digital assets:** Managing the creation, ownership, and transfer of digital products that are valuable in and of themselves or represent valuable real-world goods.

- **Digital identity:** Proving and verifying identification and authentication through the use of unique digital things.

- **Notary services:** Digitizing, archiving, and validating documents or contracts, as well as establishing proof of ownership or transfer.

- **Compliance and auditing:** Conducting audits of individuals or companies operating in regulated industries.

- **Taxation:** Calculating and collecting taxes based on transactions or single ownership, decreasing tax evasion2 and double taxation.

- **Voting:** Creating, disseminating, and tallying electronic ballot sheets.

- **Record management:** The process of creating and keeping medical records.

Chapter 5: Ether Wallets

The term "wallet" has various meanings in Ethereum. At its most basic level, a wallet is a piece of software that acts as the principal user interface for Ethereum.

The wallet maintains track of a user's keys and addresses and initiates and also signs transactions. Additionally, certain Ethereum wallets are capable of communicating with contracts, like ERC20 tokens. From a programmer's perspective, the phrase "wallet" relates to the system that stores and manages users' keys.

Each wallet has a key management component. That is the extent of most wallets. Other wallets are classified as browsers, gateways to Ethereum-based decentralized apps, or DApps. There are no apparent boundaries between the many categories often referred to as "wallets."

5.1 Crypto wallets

A crypto wallet is a type of digital wallet used to accept, transmit, and store digital currencies such as Bitcoin or Ethereum. The majority of currencies have an official wallet or a third-party wallet approved for the storage of digital money.

They would function identically to traditional leather wallets used to carry cash and credit cards in an ideal world. The main distinction is that cryptocurrency wallets are virtual. However, unlike a typical wallet, this virtual wallet displays your current balance, your most recent spending, and other information that a leather wallet cannot. As with digital apps, cryptocurrency wallets are smarter in that they combine all of the advantages of a physical wallet with additional flexibility and sophistication. With just one wallet, users may store a variety of digital currencies without ever having to worry about running out of capacity.

As a cryptocurrency investor, you should acquaint yourself with how wallets function so that once you have your tokens, trading in the ICO market will be seamless.

5.2 The Cryptocurrency Wallets' Operation

Cryptocurrency wallets operate similarly to a safety deposit box where you keep valuables such as jewels, certificates, or a will. You cannot afford to lose the key to such a box since doing so effectively results in losing ownership of the precious things contained therein.

Cryptocurrency wallets operate similarly, except that you will have a digital key instead of physical keys, colloquially referred to as a master key. These are sometimes referred to as "private keys."

They may appear difficult and intimidating at first, but with practice, you will master them. When investing in initial coin offerings (ICOs) or any other digital asset, it is critical to safeguard your wallet by safeguarding your private key. You will always require the key to access your wallet assets and allow transactions from them. Therefore, always store your key in a secure location that is quickly accessible whenever you require it.

Where to get A Cryptocurrency Wallet?

By joining up for one of the wallets, you may quickly obtain cryptocurrency wallets. The following types of cryptocurrency wallets are available:

Desktops

These are wallets that are downloaded and kept on a laptop or desktop computer, and they can be accessed only from the machine on which they were downloaded.

While desktop wallets are extremely secure, their security might be jeopardized if your computer becomes infected with a virus or is hacked. However, desktop wallets are some of the most secure wallets available.

Online wallets

This type of wallet is cloud-based, and it can be accessed from any computing device. They are handier and easier to use, but they are more vulnerable to hackers because the key is held online by a third party.

Mobiles

These wallets run on a mobile application and are extremely handy to use since they can be used anywhere to conduct ICO token-related transactions.

Hardware

Hardware wallets are distinguished from software wallets because the private key is physically saved on hardware, such as a USB device. Although transactions are still done online with a hardware wallet, there is a higher level of security with this type of wallet because everything is stored offline. The user only has to connect the hardware to an Internet-connected device from any location to conduct transactions.

Is It Better to Use a Single Currency or Multiple Currencies?

While Bitcoin is the most well-known digital money, many other currencies have developed their own infrastructure and environment. However, some good news for individuals investing in many different ICOs is that certain wallets support multiple tokens. You do not need to create a separate wallet for each coin. Instead, create a multi-currency wallet that enables you to utilize many currencies concurrently from a single wallet.

Are crypto wallets secure?

Cryptocurrency wallets have been designed to be extremely secure. However, the amount of protection varies amongst wallets. Similar to the security of your usernames and passwords, the security of your wallet is secured by adhering rigorously to the best security standards. To serve as a guide, the following are some secure wallet practices:

1. Obtain a secure wallet.

With so many cryptocurrency wallets accessible, it is prudent to find one that goes above and beyond the basic wallet supplied by most wallet providers. Some wallets now include encryption mechanisms to increase the secrecy of private keys.

2. Make advantage of the technology of cold storage

Users should have at least two wallets, but the number should vary according to the quantity of crypto they own. One wallet should be used only for transactional and trading reasons, while the other should be used exclusively for the secure storage of ICO tokens. This sort of wallet is typically referred to as a "cold storage" wallet because it is used just for storage and never participates in any transactions. Always ensure that the trading wallet has a small number of ICOs sufficient for your present trading operations.

3. WIFI Knowledge

Always use caution while visiting websites online and using a device equipped with an ICO wallet. Risky Wi-Fi and dangerous websites may jeopardize your wallet. Additionally, keep in mind that you should always watch this item and never give it to anybody.

4. Phishing

Several phishing schemes in the crypto sector use emails or Google Ads. Phishing scams are prevalent.

Therefore, always verify that the wallet firms' domains are properly indicated in the emails you get from them, and never search up their site addresses by clicking on a Google Ad.

5. Turn off any auto-updates.

You should disable automatic updates for any crypto-related programs, as most application bugs have the potential to harm the wallet owner.

6. Double-check all of the addresses.

It is always important to double-check all of the addresses you are transferring money. This is because malicious applications can copy the pattern.

5.3 Different Crypto Wallets

The number of wallets available continues to grow daily, and consumers now have a plethora of alternatives. However, before you decide on which wallet to use for your key coin offering investment, keep the following points in mind:

- Are you going to invest in many initial coin offerings (ICOs) or just one?

- Do you require access to your digital wallet from any location, or will you use it at home?

- Will you use your wallet for daily transactions, or are you more interested in purchasing and retaining coins as an investment?

After asking yourself these questions and thoroughly assessing your needs, you can easily pick which wallet would best serve your interests, allowing you to pick the most suitable wallet.

Several of the finest crypto wallets for ICO tokens include the following:

MyEtherWallet

This is one of the most widely-used wallets in the crypto community. It may purchase, trade successfully, and store ERC20 tokens received through initial coin offerings (ICOs). It is one of the most widely accepted wallets since it combines an internet wallet with an offline wallet.

Jaxx

This is another incredible wallet. It can store, trade, and control Bitcoin, Litecoin, Ethereum, Augur, and a slew of other blockchain-based assets. It allows you total control over your key, in addition to offering a slew of basic yet useful functions.

Trezor

This hardware wallet provides an extremely secure method of safeguarding your funds from hackers and malware. Its major distinguishing qualities are cross-platform compatibility and an OLED display.

KeepKey

This is another hardware wallet for Ethereum, Bitcoin, Litecoin, and other tokens. Additionally, it includes a USB port as one of its distinctive characteristics.

The Exodus

This is a multi-digital asset wallet and the first desktop wallet to include an integrated ShapeShift feature that enables easy and rapid conversion between various cryptocurrency tokens and altcoins. Additionally, it permits the storage of the private key in a configurable user interface application.

5.4 A Brief Overview of Wallet Technology

This section will discuss the various technologies used to develop user-friendly, secure, and customizable Ethereum wallets. When developing wallets, it is critical to strike a balance between convenience and privacy. The most efficient Ethereum wallet stores all of its funds with a single private key and address. Unfortunately, such a method presents a privacy nightmare since all your operations may readily be tracked. While using a unique key for every transaction increases security, it becomes incredibly complex to administer. The optimal balance is tough to attain, which is why a well-designed wallet is critical. Ethereum wallets do not hold ether or tokens, contrary to popular belief. Indeed, the wallet contains simply the keys. Ethereum's blockchain is used to store ether and other tokens. By verifying transactions only with keys in their wallets, users gain control of the network's tokens.

In some ways, an Ethereum wallet is similar to a digital keychain. However, because the wallet keys are the only item necessary to send or receive ether or tokens, this distinction is mostly unimportant in practice. The distinction is in changing one's outlook from dealing with the centralized approach of conventional banking (where only you and the financial institution can see the money in your account, and you only need to reassure the bank that you want to move funds to complete a transaction) to interacting with the decentralized network of blockchain platforms (where anyone can see an account's ether balance, even if they do not recognize who owns it, and everybody needs to be reassured that they want to) to dealing with the decentralized network of blockchain platforms (where In reality, this implies that there is a mechanism to check an account's balance without accessing the wallet. Additionally, you may migrate your existing wallet us account management to a new wallet.

Wallets are split into two categories based on the relationship between the keys they store.

- The first kind is a nondeterministic wallet, which generates each key separately using a distinct random integer.

  The keys are unrelated. This sort of wallet is often referred to as a JBOK wallet, from "Just a Bunch of Keys."

- The second form of wallet is the deterministic wallet, which derives all keys from a single master key, referred to as the seed. Each key in this form of wallet is connected to the previous one and maybe produced again if the seed is accessible.

Numerous key derivation methods are employed in deterministic wallets.

As explained in "Deterministic Hierarchical Wallets," the most often utilized derivation approach makes use of a treelike structure.

To make deterministic wallets a little more secure against data loss accidents, such as getting your mobile device stolen or accidentally dropping it in the bathroom, the seeds are regularly encoded as a series of terms (in English or another language) that you can write down and use in the event of an accident.

These are the wallet mnemonic code words. Naturally, if your mnemonic code words are hacked, they can rebuild your wallet, giving them accessibility to your ether and smart contracts. As a result, proceed with caution while constructing your list of recovery words! Never save it digitally, in a file, on a computer, or a mobile device. Make notes of it on paper and save it in a safe and secure location.

5.5 Nondeterministic Wallets

Each wallet file contains a completely random private key in the first Ethereum wallet (made for the Ethereum pre-sale). These "traditional" wallets are being dropped out in preference of deterministic wallets because of their numerous shortcomings. For example, it is best practice to avoid reusing Ethereum addresses to optimize your privacy when using Ethereum. To receive cash using a new address (needing a new private key) each time, you may go even farther and use a unique address for each transaction, but this might get costly if you regularly deal with tokens.

To adhere to this approach, a nondeterministic wallet list of keys must be increased regularly, which implies that backups must be performed frequently. If you ever lose your data (due to disk failure, a careless accident, or having your phone stolen) without first backing up your wallet, you may forfeit access to your assets and smart contracts.

Nondeterministic wallets of "type 0" are the most difficult to manage, as they produce a new wallet file for each new address "just in time." In the Keystore format, a key derivation function (KDF), sometimes called a password stretching method, is employed to guard against dictionary, brute force and rainbow table attacks. That being said, the pass does not encrypt the private key directly. Rather than that, the pass is extended by repeatedly hashing it. As specified by the Keystore JSON option crypto. Kd.params.n the hashing function is repeated 262,144 times. A brute-force attacker would have to perform 262,144 rounds of hashing to each attempted pass, considerably slowing the attack and rendering it unfeasible for sufficiently sophisticated and lengthy passes.

Numerous software libraries, such as the JavaScript library keythereum, can read and write the Keystore format. Nondeterministic wallets should not be used for anything more than rudimentary experiments. They are far too large to transport and utilize in anything but the most basic of scenarios. Instead of that, utilize an HD wallet with an industry-standard mnemonic.

5.6 Deterministic (Seeded) Wallets

Deterministic wallets, also referred to as "seeded" wallets, store private keys that are all obtained from a single key or seed. The seed is a random integer paired with other information, such as an index number or "chain code, " to generate infinite private keys because a single backup system at wallet installation time is enough to secure all funds and smart contracts in a deterministic wallet. The seed is adequate to retrieve all derived keys. Additionally, the seed is sufficient for exporting or importing a wallet, allowing for straightforward key movement between wallet implementations since just the seed is necessary to access the full wallet, seed security is crucial. On the other side, the ability to focus security efforts on a specific piece of data may be seen positively.

Hierarchical Deterministic Wallets

Deterministic wallets were designed to generate the process of creating many keys from a single seed. At the moment, the most sophisticated sort of deterministic wallet is the hierarchical deterministic (HD) wallet described by Bitcoin's BIP-32 standard. HD wallets utilize keys obtained from a tree structure, which enables a parent key to generate a chain of child keys, each of which would generate a succession of descendant keys, and so on.

In comparison to deterministic wallets, HD wallets have a few notable benefits. First, the tree structure may be utilized to convey extra organizational information, as when one line of sub keys gets incoming payments. At the same time, another branch collects change from outgoing payments.

Additionally, key branches can be employed in corporate environments, where various sections are attributed to departments, subsidiaries, specialized roles, or accounting categories.

The second benefit of HD wallets is that users may generate a sequence of public keys without knowing the private keys. This permits the usage of HD wallets on insecure servers or in a watch-only or receive-only mode, in which the wallet does not have the private keys necessary to spend the cash.

Seeds and Mnemonic Codes

There are several techniques for securely storing and retrieving a private key. The current favoured way is to utilize a series of phrases that, when combined correctly, may be used to reproduce the private key in its entirety. This is referred as mnemonic, and BIP-39 has standardized the technique.

Numerous Ethereum wallets support this standard, allowing for the import and export of backup and recovery seeds through interoperable mnemonics.

In practice, the likelihood of making errors when noting down the hex pattern is just too large. By comparison, the list of often used words is rather simple to handle, owing to the high degree of duplication in word composition (particularly English words).

Suppose the word "inzect" was unintentionally recorded. In that case, it could be readily recognized that it is not a legitimate English word and that the word "insect" should be used anyway if wallet recovery is necessary.

We are discussing a version of the seed because it is the best practice for managing HD wallets; the seed is necessary to recover a wallet in case of data loss (by accident or theft), thus maintaining a backup is critical.

However, since the seed must be kept private, digital copies should be avoided at all costs. Therefore, the previous recommendation is to back up with pen and paper.

To summarize, encoding the seed for an HD wallet with a recovery word list is the most secure method for exporting, transcribing, recording on paper, reading without error, and importing a private key set into some other wallet.

Chapter 6: Tokens

The term "token" is derived from the Old English word "tcen," which translates as "a sign or emblem." Transportation tokens, laundry tokens, and arcade game tokens are privately issued coin-like things with negligible intrinsic value.

6.1 Understanding The Concept of Tokens

Tokens managed on Blockchains are currently redefining the term to refer to blockchain based abstractions that may be held and represent assets, cash, or access rights. The link between the term "token" and little value is mostly owing to real tokens' limited use.

Physical tokens are frequently confined to certain businesses, organizations, or locations, are difficult to trade, and generally serve a single function. These limits are lifted or, more precisely, they are entirely redefinable with blockchain tokens. Numerous blockchain tokens are used globally and may be traded for one another or other currencies on worldwide liquid marketplaces. The expectation of "insignificant value" is likewise obsolete. With the limits on usage and ownership removed, the assumption of "insignificant value" is now obsolete.

What Are Tokens Used for?

The most prevalent application of tokens is digital private money. This is, however, simply one conceivable use. Tokens can perform a wide number of functions, many of which overlap. A token, for example, can simultaneously represent a voting right, an access right, and ownership of a resource.

Currency is merely the first "app," as the following list demonstrates:

Currency

A token may serve as a currency medium, with its value decided by a private transaction.

Resource

A token may represent a resource gained or created in a sharing economy or resource-sharing environment; for resources, a storage or CPU token may represent resources shared across a network.

Asset

A token may represent ownership of an intrinsic or extrinsic, tangible or intangible asset, such as gold, real estate, a car, oil, energy, or MMOG goods.

Access

A token can represent the right of access to a digital or physical asset, such as a discussion forum, an exclusive website, a hotel room, or a rental car.

Equity

A token may represent shareholder equity in a digital organization (for example, a decentralized autonomous organization) or a legal entity (for example, a corporation).

Voting

In a digital or judicial process, a token can reflect voting rights.

Collectible

A token might be digitally collectable (such as CryptoPunks) or physically collectable (such as CryptoPunks) (such as a painting)

Identity

A token may represent a digital identity (such as an avatar) or a legal identity (for example, a national ID).

Attestation

A token might represent an authority's verification or attestation of the fact or a decentralized reputation system (for example, birth certificate, a marriage record, or college degree).

Utility

Tokens can be used to pay or acquire access to services.

Frequently, many of these functions are merged into a single token.

It might be difficult to tell them apart at times because their physical manifestations have always been tightly intertwined.

For example, a driver's license (attestation) doubles as an identity document (identity) in the physical world, and the two are inextricably linked.

In the digital environment, formerly interwoven functions may be isolated and developed separately (for example, anonymous attestation).

Tokens and Fungibility

In economics, fungibility refers to the characteristic of an item or commodity whose constituent units are fundamentally interchangeable. When a single unit of a token may be replaced for another with no difference in value or function, the token is fungible. To be precise, if a token's past history can be tracked, it is not fungible. Provenance tracking enables blacklisting and whitelisting, significantly decreasing or eliminating fungibility.

Non-fungible tokens each represent a unique tangible or intangible thing and cannot thus be exchanged. For example, a token representing ownership of a certain Van Gogh artwork is not comparable to another token indicating ownership of a Picasso, even if both are part of the same "art ownership token" system.

Similarly, a cryptocurrency token representing a particular digital item, such as a CryptoKitty, cannot be swapped for another CryptoKitty. Each non-fungible token is identified uniquely by a unique identifier, such as a serial number.

Counterparty Danger

Counterparty risk means that the opposite party in a transaction may default on their commitments. Since certain transactions include more than two parties, there is extra counterparty risk. For instance, if you hold a precious metal certificate of deposit and sell it to someone, the transaction involves at least three parties: the seller, the buyer, and the custodian of the precious metal. Because someone owns the physical asset, they must become a party to the transaction's completion, which introduces counterparty risk into every transaction using that item.

In general, when an asset is traded indirectly via the exchange of a token of ownership, there is added counterparty risk from the asset's custodian.

Is the asset in their possession?

Will they recognize (or authorize) the transfer of ownership based on the transfer of a token (such as a certificate, deed, title, or digital token)? As is the case in the non-digital world, it is vital to understand who owns the underlying asset represented by the token and what regulations apply to that underlying asset in the world of digital tokens representing assets.

Tokens and Intrinsicality

The word "Intrinsic" is derived from the Latin word "intra," which means "from inside." Certain tokens reflect digital assets intrinsic to blockchain technology. Consensus rules regulate both these digital assets and the tokens themselves. This has an important consequence: tokens representing intrinsic assets are not exposed to additional counterparty risk. If you own the keys to a CryptoKitty, no one else holds them for you — you directly own it.

Consensus rules from the blockchain apply, and your ownership (i.e., control) of the private keys is equal to direct ownership of the asset. On the other hand, many tokens represent extrinsic assets like real estate, voting shares in corporations, trademarks, and gold bars. Ownership of these non-blockchain assets is regulated by law, custom, and policy, which are different from the consensus rules governing the token. In other words, token issuers and owners may continue to use non-smart contracts.

As a result, because these extrinsic assets are maintained by custodians, registered in external registries, and regulated by external laws and rules, they introduce additional counterparty risk.

The capacity to transform extrinsic assets to intrinsic assets, eliminating counterparty risk, is one of the most significant consequences of blockchain-based tokens. An excellent example is transitioning from a corporation (irrelevant) to equity or a voting token in a DAO or similar (intrinsic) organization.

Tokens: Are They for Utility or Equity?

Today, almost all Ethereum projects begin with some form of token. However, are tokens required for all of these projects? Are there any disadvantages to employing a token, or is the motto "tokenize everything" a possibility?

In principle, tokens might be the ultimate management or organizational tool. In reality, the integration of blockchain platforms, such as Ethereum, into established social systems has severely restricted their application thus far.

First, let us define the function of a token in a new project.

Tokens are often utilized in one of the two ways in most projects: "utility tokens" or "equity tokens." Frequently, these two jobs are confused. Utility tokens are required to access a service, application, or resource. Utility tokens represent resources such as shared storage or access to services such as social media networks. Equity tokens denote ownership or control of an entity, such as a startup. Equity tokens can be as basic as nonvoting shares for dividends and earnings distribution or as complicated as voting in a decentralized autonomous organization. The platform is administered via a sophisticated governance mechanism based on token holders' votes.

That is correct!

Numerous businesses have a problem: while tokens are a wonderful instrument for fundraising, issuing securities (equity) to the general public is a regulated activity in most nations.

Numerous firms intend to circumvent these legal limits by disguising equity tokens as utility tokens and conducting a public offering under the guise of a pre-sale of "service access vouchers," or utility tokens as we refer to them.

It remains to be seen if these sham equity offers can evade regulatory scrutiny.

As the ancient adage goes, "If it walks and quacks like a duck, it is a duck." Regulators are unlikely to be diverted by these semantic twists; rather, they are more likely to view such legal ambiguity as an attempt to deceive the public.

Tokens for Utility Tokens: Who Needs Them?

The issue is that utility tokens pose major risks and impediments to startup adoption. Perhaps "tokenize everything" will become a reality in the far future. Still, the set of individuals who understand and desire to utilize a token is a subset of the already limited cryptocurrency market.

Each invention entails a degree of risk and serves as a market filter for a business. Innovation entails breaking from established practices and choosing the less-travelled path. Already, this is a lonely stroll. It is a lonely route for a startup to take when attempting to innovate in a new technology field, such as storage sharing via peer-to-peer networks. Adding a utility token to the invention and asking users to adopt tokens to utilize the service, the risk is compounded, and the adoption barriers are raised.

It deviates from the already isolated road of peer-to-peer storage innovation and heads into the wilderness.

Consider each advancement as a filter.

It limits adoption to those segments of the market that can be early adopters of the invention. This impact is exacerbated by adding a second filter, thus restricting the addressable market. You are asking your early adopters to embrace not one but two unique technologies: the novel application/platform/service you invented and the token economy.

Each innovation carries risk, increasing the likelihood of the startup failing. When you add a utility token to an existing high-risk firm, you add all of the risks associated with the underlying platform (Ethereum), the larger economy (exchanges, liquidity), the regulatory environment (equity and commodities regulators), and technology (smart contracts, token standards). That is a huge risk for a company.

Advocates of "tokenize everything" would almost certainly claim that they will inherit the token economy's market fervor, early adopters, technology, innovation, and liquidity by embracing tokens.

Additionally, this is right. The question is whether the benefits and exhilaration of adventure exceed the risks and uncertainty. Nonetheless, the crypto sphere is home to some of the most inventive business models.

Suppose regulators do not move swiftly enough to embrace new rules and promote new business models. In that case, entrepreneurs and their associated talent will seek to operate in more crypto-friendly countries.

Finally, when we explored tokens at the chapter's outset, we discussed the common definition of "token" as "something of negligible value."

The fundamental reason for the low value of most tokens is that they are limited to a single use: one bus company, one laundry, one arcade, one hotel, or one corporate shop. Due to low liquidity, restricted application, and high conversion fees, the value of tokens is reduced to "token" value.

When you include a utility token into your platform but restrict its use to your single platform with a tiny market, you are re-creating the conditions that rendered real tokens useless. This may be the optimal way for tokenization integration in your project.

If, on the other hand, a user needs to change anything into your utility token to utilize your platform and then convert the remaining back into something more generally valuable, you have produced a corporate scrip.

While the switching costs of a digital token are orders of magnitude less than those of a physical token with no market, they are not zero.

Utility tokens that may be utilized in various businesses will be quite intriguing and, in all likelihood, pretty lucrative. However, if you founded your business intending to bootstrap a whole industry-standard to flourish, you may have already done so.

Without a token, a token cannot work. Adopt it because the token eliminates a significant market barrier or resolves an access issue. Avoid using a utility token since it is the only method to acquire funds swiftly, and you must pretend that the offering is not a public securities offering.

6.2 The ERC20 Token

Before Ethereum, there were blockchain tokens. In some senses, Bitcoin, the first blockchain money, is a token in and of itself. Numerous token platforms were also established on Bitcoin and other cryptocurrencies before Ethereum. However, adopting the first token standard on Ethereum resulted in a proliferation of tokens.

Tokens are one of the most apparent and practical uses of a universal programmable blockchain like Ethereum, according to Buterin. Indeed, it was typical to see Vitalik and others wearing T-shirts with the Ethereum logo and a sample smart contract on the back during Ethereum's first year. This T-shirt came in various styles, but the most popular included a token implementation. Before we go into the mechanics of producing tokens on Ethereum, it is critical to understand how tokens function on the platform.Tokens are distinct from ether in that the Ethereum protocol does not know of them. While transmitting ether is a built-in feature of the Ethereum network, sending or even possessing tokens is not. Ethereum accounts' ether balances are managed at the protocol level, whilst their token balances are managed at the smart contract level.

To create a new token on Ethereum, you must first create a new smart contract. Once implemented, the smart contract takes care of everything, including ownership, transfers, and access permissions. You may create your smart contract in any way you choose, but it is usually prudent to adhere to an existing standard. Following that, we shall examine such norms.

ERC20 Token Standard

The initial standard was proposed in November 2015 by Fabian Vogelsteller as an Ethereum Request for Comments (ERC). It was immediately allocated GitHub issue number 20, giving it the moniker "ERC20 token." Currently, the great majority of tokens adhere to the ERC20 standard.

The ERC20 request for comments evolved into Ethereum Improvement Proposal 20 (EIP-20). However, it is still commonly known by its original designation, ERC20.

ERC20 is a standard for fungible tokens, which means that various units of an ERC20 token are interchangeable and lack any unique attributes. The ERC20 standard specifies a standardized interface for token-implemented contracts that enables any compatible token to be accessed and used in the same way.

The interface comprises several required functions and properties and certain optional functions and attributes that developers may add.

ERC20-required functions and events

A token contract that is ERC20 complaint must provide the following functions and events:

totalSupply

Returns the total number of units of this token that are presently in existence.

ERC20 tokens can have a fixed or variable supply.

balanceOf

Returns the address's token balance when given an address.

transfer

Given an address and an amount, transfers that amount of tokens to that address from the balance of the address that initiated the transfer.

transferfrom

It transfers tokens from one account to another given a sender, receiver, and amount.

approve

When used in combination with approval, given a destination address and an amount, it enables that address to execute numerous transfers up to that amount from the account that issued the approval.

allowance

Returns the spender's remaining amount and is authorized to withdraw from the owner given an owner address and a spender address.

Transfer

An event triggered on successful transfer (call to transfer or transferFrom) (even for zero-value transfers).

Approval

An approval event is registered when a call to approve is successful.

ERC20 functions that are optional

Along with the mandatory functions stated before, the standard also defines the following optional functions:

Name

Returns the token's human-readable name (e.g., "US Dollars").

Symbol

Returns a token's human-readable symbol (e.g., "USD").

Decimals

Returns the number of decimals used to split token values.

For instance, if it equals two decimals, the token's value is divided by 100 to obtain its user representation.

The ERC20 interface defined in Solidity.

This is how an ERC20 interface specification appears in Solidity:

```
contract ERC20 {
    function totalSupply() constant returns (uint theTotalSupply);
    function balanceOf(address _owner) constant returns (uint balance);
    function transfer(address _to, uint _value) returns (bool success);
    function transferFrom(address _from, address _to, uint _value) returns (bool success);
    function approve(address _spender, uint _value) returns (bool success);
    function allowance(address _owner, address _spender) constant returns (uint remaining);
    event Transfer(address indexed _from, address indexed _to, uint _value);
    event Approval(address indexed _owner, address indexed _spender, uint _value); }
```

ERC20-compliant data structures

If you examine any ERC20 implementation, you will discover that it uses two distinct data structures: one to track balances and another to track allowances. They are implemented via data mapping in Solidity.

The initial data mapping builds an internal database that organizes token balances by owner. The token contract may then keep track of which parties own tokens. Each transfer results in reducing funds from one balance and the addition of funds to another.

```
mapping(address        =>        uint256)  balances;
```

The second data structure is an allowances data map.

As we shall see in the next section, an ERC20 token owner can delegate authority to a spender, enabling them to spend a certain amount (allowance) from the owner's balance.

Allowances are managed by the ERC20 contract using a two-dimensional mapping, with the primary key being the token owner's address, which is mapped to a spender address and an allowance amount.

```
mapping    (address =>    mapping (address =>    uint256)) public    allowed;
```

ERC20 workflows: "transfer" and "approve & transferFrom"

ERC20 is capable of supporting two separate processes.

The first is a straightforward workflow that utilizes the transfer function.

This is the workflow through which wallets transfer tokens to other wallets.

The vast majority of token transactions occur during the transfer workflow.

The transferred contract is quite simple to execute.

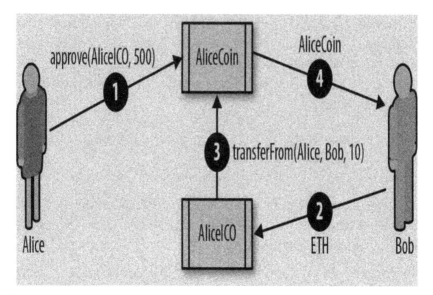

If Alice intends to give Bob ten tokens, her wallet launches a transaction to the address of the token contract, running the transfer function with Bob's address and ten as inputs.

The token contract deducts ten dollars from Alice's balance (–10) and adds ten dollars to Bob's balance (+10), triggering a transfer event.

The second workflow consists of two transactions: authorize and transferFrom.

A token owner can assign control to another address using this workflow.

It is most frequently used to delegate control over token distribution to a contract, although exchanges can also utilize it. For instance, if a corporation wants to sell tokens during an initial coin offering (ICO), they can authorize a crowdsale contract address to release a certain number of tokens. The crowdsale contract can then transfer the balance of the token contract owner to each token buyer.

ICOs

Initial Coin Offerings (ICOs) are a sort of crowdfunding in which businesses and organizations raise money via the sale of tokens. The term originates from the phrase "initial public offering," which refers to the procedure through which a public firm sells shares to investors on a stock market. Compared to the highly controlled initial public offering (IPO) markets, ICOs are unregulated, worldwide, and anarchic.

The examples and explanations of ICOs in this book are not intended to endorse this fundraising method.

Two transactions are required to complete the approve and transfer workflow.

Consider Alice's desire to approve the AliceICO contract to sell 50% of all AliceCoin tokens to purchasers Bob and Charlie.

Alice uses the AliceCoin ERC20 contract to send AliceCoin to her address.

The AliceICO contract is then launched, which allows for the sale of tokens in exchange for ether. Alice then initiates the workflow for approval and transfer.

She sends a transaction to the AliceCoin contract, indicating that it has been authorized and including the AliceICO contract's address and 50% of the total supply as arguments.

This initiates the approval event. The AliceICO contract now can sell AliceCoin and must refund some AliceCoin to Bob when it gets ether from Bob. The AliceICO contract includes an exchange rate between AliceCoin and ether.

Alice's exchange rate when she formed the AliceICO contract dictates how many tokens Bob receives in return for the ether contributed to the AliceICO contract.

When the AliceICO contract calls the AliceCoin transferFrom function, it sets Alice's address as the sender and Bob's address as the receiver. It then uses the exchange rate to determine the number of AliceCoin tokens to transfer to Bob in the value field.

By moving the balance from Alice's address to Bob's address, the AliceCoin contract initiates a transfer event. The AliceICO contract may be invoked indefinitely many times if Alice's approval limit is not exceeded. The AliceICO contract can keep track of how many AliceCoin tokens it may sell by using the allowance method.

Issues associated with ERC20 Tokens

The adoption of the ERC20 token standard has been extremely phenomenal. Thousands of tokens have been issued to test new features and collect revenue via different "crowdfunding" auctions and initial coin offerings (ICOs). However, as with the issue of sending tokens to contract addresses, there are a few possible stumbling blocks.

One of the subtler difficulties with ERC20 tokens is that they emphasize the distinctions between tokens and ether. When ether is transferred via a transaction with a recipient address as its destination, token transfers occur within the particular token contract state and have the token contract as their destination, not the receiver's address. The token contract maintains balances and broadcasts events. During a token transfer, no transaction is issued to the token recipient. Rather, the recipient's address is added to a map included within the token contract. A transaction that transfers ether to an address modifies the status of the address. A transaction that transfers a token to an address does not affect the recipient address.

Even if a wallet supports ERC20 tokens, it will be unaware of a token balance unless the user specifically adds a token contract to "monitor."

Certain wallets monitor the most popular token contracts for balances held by addresses under their control, although this is only true for a tiny portion of extant ERC20 contracts.

Indeed, it is improbable that a user would choose to maintain track of the balances of all potential ERC20 token contracts. Numerous ERC20 tokens are more akin to email spam than to functional tokens. To entice users, they automatically create balances for recently active accounts. If you have an Ethereum address with a long history of activity, especially one formed during the pre-sale, it will be brimming with "junk" tokens that emerged out of nowhere. Of course, the address is not filled with tokens; the address is included within the token contracts.

These balances are only viewable if the block explorer or wallet used to see your address monitors the token contracts. Tokens do not act like ether. The send function transfers ether to any contract's payment function or externally owned address. Tokens are transferred using the Transferor, approve & transfer. Functions exclusive to the ERC20 contract and do not activate any payable functions in the recipient contract (at least in ERC20).

While tokens are designed to operate similarly to cryptocurrencies such as ether, several distinctions remove that illusion.

Consider another example.

You must first pay gas using ether to transfer or utilize ether or any Ethereum contract. Additionally, ether is required to send tokens. A token cannot be used to pay for the gas associated with a transaction, and the token contract cannot pay for the gas for you. This may change in the far future, but it can result in some unusual user experiences in the meanwhile.

Assume you are converting some bitcoin to a token via an exchange like ShapeShift. The token is "received" in a wallet, which manages the token's contract and displays your balance. It looks to be one of your wallets with other cryptocurrencies. When you attempt to transmit the token, your wallet will inform you that the transaction requires ether. You may be puzzled that you did not require ether to obtain the token. Perhaps you lack ether.

Perhaps you were unaware that the token was an Ethereum-based ERC20 token; perhaps you imagined it was a coin with its blockchain. The illusion has just been shattered. Several of these issues are specific to ERC20 tokens. Others are broader concerns about Ethereum's abstraction and interface boundaries.

Some of these issues can be resolved by altering the token interface. In contrast, others may need modifications to Ethereum's basic architecture (such as distinguishing between EOAs and contracts and between transactions and messages).

Certain problems may not be precisely "solvable," necessitating the use of user interface design to obscure the subtleties and maintain a uniform user experience regardless of the underlying disparities.

6.3 Launching Our Own ERC20 Token

Our Own ERC20 Token Is Being Launched

Let us create and launch our cryptocurrency.

In this example, we will utilize the Truffle framework.

This example assumes that you have previously installed and configured truffle and are acquainted with its basic functionality (see "Truffle").

Our token will be called the "My Ethereum Token," its symbol will be "MET."

To begin, create and establish a directory for the Truffle project.

Execute the following four programs and allow the default responses to any questions:

```
$ mkdir METoken
$ cd METoken
METoken $ truffle init
METoken $ npm init
```

The directory structure should now look like the following:

```
METoken/
+---- contracts
|    `---- Migrations.sol
+---- migrations
|    `---- 1_initial_migration.js
+---- package.json
+---- test
+---- truffle-config.js
`---- truffle.js
```

To set up your Truffle environment, modify the truffle.js and truffle-config.js configuration files, or copy them from the source.

If you are using the truffle-config.js example, add a file.env in the METoken directory that includes your test keys for implementation and testing on public Ethereum test platforms like Ropsten and Kovan.

Exporting your test network's private key is possible using MetaMask.

```
METoken/
+---- contracts
|     `---- Migrations.sol
+---- migrations
|     `---- 1_initial_migration.js
+---- package.json
+---- test
+---- truffle-config.js
+---- truffle.js
`---- .env *new file*
```

For our scenario, we will use the OpenZeppelin framework, which has many critical security tests and is extensible:

```
$ npm install openzeppelin-solidity@1.12.0
```

```
+ openzeppelin-solidity@1.12.0
added 1 package from 1 contributor and audited 2381 packages in 4.074s
```

The package openzeppelin-solidity will update roughly 250 components in the node modules directory.

Although the OpenZeppelin library provides significantly more than most ERC20 tokens, we will utilize a subset of it.

Now, let us build the contract for our token.

Make a new file named METOKEN.sol and put the GitHub sample code inside.

Because our contract, presented in Example 10-1, derives all of its features from the OpenZeppelin package, it is straightforward.

A Solidity contract that implements an ERC20 token is METoken.sol.

The optional variables title, symbols, and decimals are defined in this section.

Additionally, we establish an initialsupply variable with a value of 2.1 billion tokens and subdivide it into two decimal places for a total of 2.1 billion units.

In the contract's activation (constructor) function, we adjust the totalSupply to match the initialsupply and assign the full initialsupply to the sum of the account (msg.sender) used to build the METOKEN contract.

We are now using truffle to build the METOKEN code.

```
$ truffle compile
Compiling ./contracts/METoken.sol...
Compiling ./contracts/Migrations.sol...
Compiling openzeppelin-solidity/contracts/math/SafeMath.sol...
Compiling openzeppelin-solidity/contracts/token/ERC20/BasicToken.sol...
Compiling openzeppelin-solidity/contracts/token/ERC20/ERC20.sol...
Compiling openzeppelin-solidity/contracts/token/ERC20/ERC20Basic.sol...
Compiling openzeppelin-solidity/contracts/token/ERC20/StandardToken.sol...
```

As can be seen, truffle includes and builds the OpenZeppelin libraries' dependencies.

Let us begin by developing a migration script for the METOKEN contract's deployment.

Create a new file named 2 deploy contracts.js in the METOKEN/migrations subfolder.

Take the following code from the sample provided in the GitHub repository:

2_deploy_contracts: Migration to deploy METoken

```
link:code/truffle/METoken/migrations/2_deploy_contracts.js[]
```

Let us begin by creating a local blockchain to verify everything before deploying to any of the Ethereum test channels.

Initiate the ganache database from the command line using ganache-cli or via the user - interface with the ganache-cli command.

Once ganache is operational, we can verify that everything is working well using our METOKEN contract:

```
$ truffle migrate --network ganache
Using network 'ganache'.


Running migration: 1_initial_migration.js
  Deploying Migrations...
    ... 0xb2e90a056dc6ad8e654683921fc613c796a03b89df6760ec1db1084ea4a084eb
  Migrations: 0x8cdaf0cd259887258bc13a92c0a6da92698644c0
Saving successful migration to network...
    ... 0xd7bc86d31bee32fa3988f1c1eabce403a1b5d570340a3a9cdba53a472ee8c956
Saving artifacts...
Running migration: 2_deploy_contracts.js
  Deploying METoken...
    ... 0xbe9290d59678b412e60ed6aefedb17364f4ad2977cfb2076b9b8ad415c5dc9f0
  METoken: 0x345ca3e014aaf5dca488057592ee47305d9b3e10
Saving successful migration to network...
    ... 0xf36163615f41ef7ed8f4a8f192149a0bf633fe1a2398ce001bf44c43dc7bdda0
Saving artifacts...
```

As seen in METoken deployment on ganache, our deployment should create four new transactions on the ganache console.

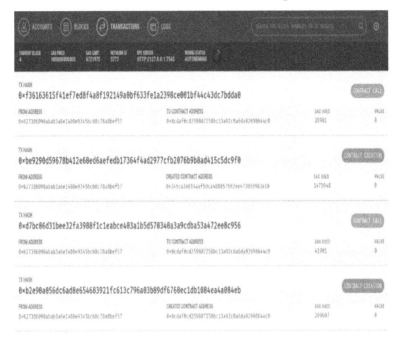

METoken interaction through the Truffle console

We can communicate with our contract on the ganache blockchain using the Truffle console. This interactive JavaScript environment allows access to the Truffle environment and the blockchain through web3. In this instance, we will link the Truffle console to the ganache blockchain as follows:

```
$ truffle console --network ganache
truffle(ganache)>
```

The truffle(ganache)> prompt indicates that we have connected to the ganache blockchain and are prepared to issue commands. Because the Truffle console supports all truffle commands, we can build and migrate directly from it. Given that we have previously executed those instructions, let us move on. Within the Truffle environment, the METoken contract resides as a JavaScript object. At the prompt, type **METoken** to dump the complete contract definition:

```
truffle(ganache)> METoken
{ [Function: TruffleContract]
  _static_methods:

[...]

currentProvider:
 HttpProvider {
    host: 'http://localhost:7545',
    timeout: 0,
    user: undefined,
    password: undefined,
    headers: undefined,
    send: [Function],
    sendAsync: [Function],
    _alreadyWrapped: true },
 network_id: '5777' }
```

Additionally, the METoken object exposes various characteristics, including the contract's address (as deployed by the migrate command):

```
truffle(ganache)> METoken.address
'0x345ca3e014aaf5dca488057592ee47305d9b3e10'
```

To communicate with the deployed contract, we must make an asynchronous call using a JavaScript "promise." We get the contract object using the deployed function and then call the totalSupply method:

```
truffle(ganache)> METoken.deployed().then(instance => instance.totalSupply())
BigNumber { s: 1, e: 9, c: [ 2100000000 ] }
```

Following that, let us verify our METoken balance and transfer some METoken to some other address using the accounts generated by ganache. To begin, let us obtain the account addresses:

```
truffle(ganache)> let accounts
undefined
truffle(ganache)> web3.eth.getAccounts((err,res) => { accounts = res })
undefined
truffle(ganache)> accounts[0]
'0x627306090abab3a6e1400e9345bc60c78a8bef57'
```

The accounts list now includes all of the ganache's accounts, with account[0] being the account that deployed the METoken contract. It should have a METoken balance since our METoken constructor distributes the whole token supply to the address that generated it. Let us verify:

```
truffle(ganache)> METoken.deployed().then(instance =>
              { instance.balanceOf(accounts[0]).then(console.log) })
undefined
truffle(ganache)> BigNumber { s: 1, e: 9, c: [ 2100000000 ] }
```

Finally, use the contract's transfer function to send 1000.00 METoken from account[0] to account[1].

```
truffle(ganache)> METoken.deployed().then(instance =>
                  { instance.transfer(accounts[1], 100000) })
undefined
truffle(ganache)> METoken.deployed().then(instance =>
                  { instance.balanceOf(accounts[0]).then(console.log) })
undefined
truffle(ganache)> BigNumber { s: 1, e: 9, c: [ 20999000000 ] }
undefined
truffle(ganache)> METoken.deployed().then(instance =>
                  { instance.balanceOf(accounts[1]).then(console.log) })
undefined
truffle(ganache)> BigNumber { s: 1, e: 5, c: [ 100000 ] }
```

As you can see, account[0] now has 20,999,000 MET, whereas account[1] only has 1,000 MET.

Switching to the ganache graphical user interface, as seen in METoken transfer on ganache, reveals the transaction that invoked the transfer function.

Using ERC20 tokens to send funds to contract addresses

So far, we have created an ERC20 token and moved several tokens across accounts. All accounts used in these demos are externally owned, which means they are managed by a private key rather than a contract. What happens if we send MET to an address specified in the contract? Let us ascertain!

To begin, let us create another contract and deploy it to our test environment. In this example, we will utilize our first contract, Faucet.sol. Let us copy it to the contacts directory of the METoken project. Our directory should seem as follows:

```
METoken/
+---- contracts
|   +---- Faucet.sol
|   +---- METoken.sol
|   `---- Migrations.sol
```

Additionally, we will add a migration to allow Faucet to be deployed independently of METoken:

```
var Faucet = artifacts.require("Faucet");


module.exports = function(deployer) {
  // Deploy the Faucet contract as our only task
  deployer.deploy(Faucet);
};
```

Let us begin by compiling and migrating the contracts directly from the Truffle console:

```
$ truffle console --network ganache
truffle(ganache)> compile
Compiling ./contracts/Faucet.sol...
Writing artifacts to ./build/contracts

truffle(ganache)> migrate
Using network 'ganache'.

Running migration: 1_initial_migration.js
  Deploying Migrations...
  ... 0x89f6a7bd2a596829c60a483ec99665c7af71e68c77a417fab503c394fcd7a0c9
  Migrations: 0xa1ccce36fb823810e729dce293b75f40fb6ea9c9
Saving artifacts...
Running migration: 2_deploy_contracts.js
  Replacing METoken...
  ... 0x28d0da26f48765f67e133e99dd275fac6a25fdfec6594060fd1a0e09a99b44ba
  METoken: 0x7d6bf9d5914d37bcba9d46df7107e71c59f3791f
Saving artifacts...
Running migration: 3_deploy_faucet.js
  Deploying Faucet...
  ... 0x6fbf283bcc97d7c52d92fd91f6ac02d565f5fded483a6a0f824f66edc6fa90c3
  Faucet: 0xb18a42e9468f7f1342fa3c329ec339f254bc7524
Saving artifacts...
```

Great. Now, let us transfer a little amount of MET to the
Faucet contract:

```
truffle(ganache)> METoken.deployed().then(instance =>
                { instance.transfer(Faucet.address, 100000) })
truffle(ganache)> METoken.deployed().then(instance =>
                { instance.balanceOf(Faucet.address).then(console.log)})
truffle(ganache)> BigNumber { s: 1, e: 5, c: [ 100000 ] }
```

Accepted, 1,000 MET have been transferred to the Faucet contract. How do we now get those tokens?

Remember, Faucet.

Sol is a rather straightforward contract. It has a single function, withdraws, used to withdraw ether. It lacks a withdrawal option for MET or any other ERC20 token. If we use it to withdraw, it will attempt to transmit ether but fail due to the Faucet's lack of ether balance.

The METoken contract knows that Faucet has a balance, but it cannot transfer that amount until it gets a transfer call from the contract's address. We need to invoke the transfer method in METoken from the Faucet contract somehow.

If you are unsure what to do next, refrain. There is no way to resolve this issue. The MET sent to Faucet is permanently stuck. Only the Faucet contract can transfer it, and the Faucet contract lacks the code necessary to invoke an ERC20 token contract's transfer function.

Perhaps you foresaw this issue. Almost certainly, you did not. Indeed, neither did hundreds of Ethereum users who transferred different tokens mistakenly to contracts that lacked ERC20 functionality. According to some estimations, tokens worth over USD 2.5 billion (at the time of writing) have been "stuck" in this manner and are now permanently gone.One possibility for ERC20 tokens to lose their tokens mistakenly during a transfer is when they try to move to exchange or another service. They copy an Ethereum address from an exchange's website, mistakenly believing that they may transfer tokens to it directly.

On the other hand, numerous exchanges advertise receiving addresses that are genuine contracts! These contracts are designed to accept only ether, not ERC20 tokens, and often sweep all monies received to "cold storage" or another controlled wallet. Despite several cautions to "do not transfer tokens to this address," many tokens are lost in this manner.

Demonstrating the workflow "approve & transferFrom"

Our Faucet contract was unable to process ERC20 tokens. Using the transfer function to send tokens to it resulted in the loss of those tokens. Let us now rebuild the contract to support ERC20 tokens. We will convert it into a faucet that will provide MET to everyone who requests it.

We will create a clone of the truffle project directory (named METoken METFaucet), start truffle and npm, install the OpenZeppelin dependencies, and copy the METoken.sol contract in this example. See our first example, Launching Our Own ERC20 Token, for complete steps.

METFaucet.Sol is our new faucet contract, and it will resemble METFaucet.

```
link:code/truffle/METoken_METFaucet/contracts/METFaucet.sol[]
```

We have modified the simple Faucet example quite a bit. METFaucet will need two more variables due to its usage of the transferFrom function in METoken. One will include the address of the METoken contract that has been deployed. The other will have the owner of the MET's address, who will allow faucet withdrawals. METFaucet will invoke METoken.transferFrom and order it to transfer MET from the owner to the address associated with the faucet withdrawal request.

These two variables are declared here:

```
StandardToken public METoken;
address public METOwner;
```

Since our faucet must be initialized with the necessary METoken and METOwner addresses, we must define a custom constructor:

```
// METFaucet constructor - provide the address of the METoken contract and
// the owner address we will be approved to transferFrom
function METFaucet(address _METoken, address _METOwner) public {

        // Initialize the METoken from the address provided
        METoken = StandardToken(_METoken);
        METOwner = _METOwner;
}
```

The next modification will be to the withdrawal feature. Rather of calling transfer, METFaucet makes advantage of METoken's transferFrom function to request that MET be sent to the faucet recipient:

```
// Use the transferFrom function of METoken
METoken.transferFrom(METOwner, msg.sender, withdraw_amount);
```

Finally, since our faucet is no longer delivering ether, we should probably prohibit anybody from sending ether to METFaucet, as we do not want it to get stuck. We modify the fallback payable method to refuse to receive ether, reverting any incoming payments using the reverse function:

```
// REJECT any incoming ether
function () public payable { revert(); }
```

After completing the METFaucet.sol code, we will need to alter the migration script to deploy it. This migration script will be a little more involved since METFaucet is dependent on the METoken address. We will utilize a JavaScript promise to deploy the two contracts sequentially. Create the following file: 2 deploy contracts.js

```
var METoken = artifacts.require("METoken");
var METFaucet = artifacts.require("METFaucet");
var owner = web3.eth.accounts[0];


module.exports = function(deployer) {


        // Deploy the METoken contract first
        deployer.deploy(METoken, {from: owner}).then(function() {
                // Then deploy METFaucet and pass the address of METoken and the
                // address of the owner of all the MET who will approve METFaucet
                return deployer.deploy(METFaucet, METoken.address, owner);
        });
}
```

Now that everything is configured, we can test it in the Truffle console. To begin, we deploy the contracts through migrating. When METoken is deployed, it will assign all MET to the web3.eth.accounts[0] account that generated it. Then, we use METoken's approve function to provide METFaucet permission to transmit up to 1,000 MET on behalf of web3.eth.accounts[0]. Finally, we call METFaucet.remove from web3.eth.accounts[1] to attempt to withdraw ten MET. The console instructions are as follows:

```
$ truffle console --network ganache
truffle(ganache)> migrate
Using network 'ganache'.

Running migration: 1_initial_migration.js
  Deploying Migrations...
  ... 0x79352b43e18cc46b023a779e9a0d16b30f127bfa40266c02f9871d63c26542c7
  Migrations: 0xaa588d3737b611bafd7bd713445b314bd453a5c8
Saving artifacts...
Running migration: 2_deploy_contracts.js
  Replacing METoken...
  ... 0xc42a57f22cddf95f6f8c19d794c8af3b2491f568b38b96fef15b13b6e8bfff21
  METoken: 0xf204a4ef082f5c04bb89f7d5e6568b796096735a
  Replacing METFaucet...
  ... 0xd9615cae2fa4f1e8a377de87f86162832cf4d31098779e6e00df1ae7f1b7f864
  METFaucet: 0x75c35c980c0d37ef46df04d31a140b65503c0eed
Saving artifacts...
truffle(ganache)> METoken.deployed().then(instance =>
              { instance.approve(METFaucet.address, 100000) })
truffle(ganache)> METoken.deployed().then(instance =>
              { instance.balanceOf(web3.eth.accounts[1]).then(console.log) })
truffle(ganache)> BigNumber { s: 1, e: 0, c: [ 0 ] }
truffle(ganache)> METFaucet.deployed().then(instance =>
              { instance.withdraw(1000, {from:web3.eth.accounts[1]}) } )
truffle(ganache)> METoken.deployed().then(instance =>
              { instance.balanceOf(web3.eth.accounts[1]).then(console.log) })
truffle(ganache)> BigNumber { s: 1, e: 3, c: [ 1000 ] }
```

The results show that we can utilize the approve & transferFrom procedure to authorize the transfer of tokens specified in one contract to another. ERC20 tokens may be used in EOAs and other contracts if utilized appropriately.

However, properly handling ERC20 tokens is shifted to the user interface. If a user transfers ERC20 tokens to a contract address that is not prepared to handle ERC20 tokens, the tokens are lost.

6.4 The ERC721 Non-Fungible Tokens (NFT) Standard

All of the token standards examined so far are fungible, implying that token units are interchangeable. The ERC20 token standard tracks just the final balance of each account and does not track (explicitly) the origin of every token. ERC721 is a standard for non-fungible tokens, commonly referred to as deeds.

According to the Oxford Dictionary, a deed is a legally binding document that has been signed and delivered, typically relating to property ownership or legal rights. The term "deed" is used to represent "property ownership," even though they are not yet considered "legal papers" in any state.

Legal ownership based on digital signatures on a blockchain network is likely to be recognized legally at some time in the future. Tokens that are not fungible are used to track ownership of one-of-a-kind items. The thing possessed can be a digital item, such as an in-game item or digital collectable, or a physical item, such as a house, a car, or an artwork, the ownership of which is tracked by a token. Deeds can also represent loans (debt), liens, easements, and other objects with a negative value.

The ERC721 standard imposes no constraints or expectations on the nature of the item whose ownership is tracked by a deed. It simply requires to be uniquely recognized, which is achieved via a 256-bit identification in this standard.

The information and discussion of the standard are maintained in two locations on GitHub:

- Initial proposition

- Continued discussion

To see the essential distinction between ERC20 and ERC721, examine the ERC721 internal data structure:

```
// Mapping from deed ID to owner
mapping (uint256 => address) private deedOwner;
```

ERC721 keeps track of each deed ID and who owns it, in contrast to ERC20, which keeps track of each owner's balances, with the owner serving as the main key for the mapping.

All of the non-fungible token's attributes come from this basic distinction. ERC721's contract interface standard is as follows:

```
interface ERC721 /* is ERC165 */ {
    event Transfer(address indexed _from, address indexed _to, uint256 _deedId);
    event Approval(address indexed _owner, address indexed _approved, uint256 _deedId);
    event ApprovalForAll(address indexed _owner, address indexed _operator, bool _approved);

    function balanceOf(address _owner) external view returns (uint256 _balance);
    function ownerOf(uint256 _deedId) external view returns (address _owner);
    function transfer(address _to, uint256 _deedId) external payable;
    function transferFrom(address _from, address _to, uint256 _deedId) external payable;
    function approve(address _approved, uint256 _deedId) external payable;
    function setApprovalForAll(address _operateor, boolean _approved) payable;
    function supportsInterface(bytes4 interfaceID) external view returns (bool); }
```

Additionally, ERC721 supports two optional interfaces: one for metadata management and another for deed and owner enumeration.

The ERC721 optional interface for

```
interface ERC721Metadata /* is ERC721 */ {
    function name() external pure returns (string _name);
    function symbol() external pure returns (string _symbol);
    function deedUri(uint256 _deedId) external view returns (string _deedUri); }
```

metadata is:

The ERC721 optional interface for enumeration is:

```
interface ERC721Enumerable /* is ERC721 */ {
    function totalSupply() external view returns (uint256 _count);
    function deedByIndex(uint256 _index) external view returns (uint256 _deedId);
    function countOfOwners() external view returns (uint256 _count);
    function ownerByIndex(uint256 _index) external view returns (address _owner);
    function deedOfOwnerByIndex(address _owner, uint256 _index) external view
        returns (uint256 _deedId); }
```

6.5 Some More Insight into NFTs

We are in the wild west of NFTs, where practically anything is permissible. On NFT markets, digital art, songs, jokes, recipes, and even entire enterprises are now for sale. At the moment, there are minimal constraints on the type of content that may be "tokenized" and converted into an NFT.

Because the technology is still in its infancy, this is an excellent opportunity to explore with the medium for your own work, particularly as the market and demand for digital art continue to increase. A self-evident guideline is to avoid converting copyrighted content or assets into NFTs.

What am I going to need to get started producing NFTs?

You do not need substantial expertise of crypto to construct an NFT, but a few tools, such as a crypto wallet and Ethereum, are necessary to get started. If these terms are unfamiliar to you, that is acceptable. You can configure anything from your phone in a few minutes.

In this part, I will walk you through the process of creating a crypto wallet, purchasing Ethereum, and connecting your wallet to an NFT marketplace.

- Create an Ethereum Wallet
- Acquire a small quantity of Ethereum
- Connect your wallet to a NFT marketplace.

The First Step is to Create an Ethereum Wallet.

The first step on your NFT journey is to construct a digital wallet to securely store the crypto money needed to purchase, sell, and manufacture NFTs. Additionally, the wallet enables secure sign-in and account creation on NFT markets.

There are hundreds of platforms that offer free cryptocurrency wallets, and each of the solutions listed here is guaranteed to operate with the majority of significant NFT marketplaces and blockchain applications.

Coinbase Wallet

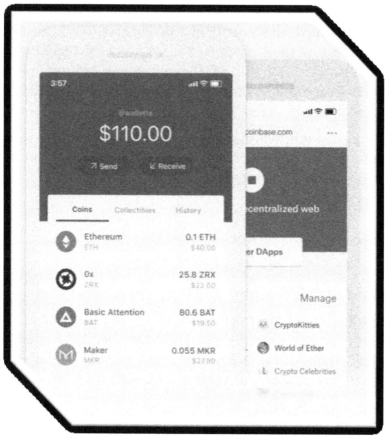

Coinbase is an excellent wallet for beginners.

Coinbase is one of the major cryptocurrency exchanges available today, and its wallet provides an excellent introduction to the world of virtual money for individuals who are unfamiliar with it. Coinbase was the first platform I used to purchase cryptocurrencies, and I can attest to how straightforward it is to get started here.

MetaMask

Metamask is a cryptocurrency wallet that is accessible as a browser extension and a mobile application. Metamask is a wallet that is used by over one million crypto enthusiasts worldwide. The wallet integrates seamlessly with the majority of crypto applications and NFT markets, and is accessible on iOS and Android as a browser extension and mobile app. Additionally, Metamask streamlines the process of acquiring crypto, eliminating the need to utilize other apps.

Rainbow

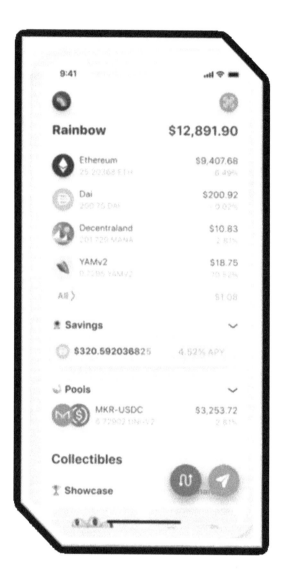

Currently, the Rainbow wallet is accessible for iOS and Android.

Rainbow is a very new wallet designed specifically for Ethereum assets. This means that you cannot keep bitcoin here, but this will not be an issue for NFTs. I adore the elegant style of this wallet and the ease with which you can display your NFT collection. Rainbow allows purchasing Ethereum on iOS as simple as using Apple Pay.

Step 2: Purchase a small quantity of Ethereum

There are expenses connected with converting your content to an NFT on the majority of big digital art markets and you will need to acquire some Ethereum (ETH) to pay the price of building your first NFT.

Ethereum's price varies minute by minute and might be difficult to follow. The simplest method to get started is to select a dollar amount that you are prepared to invest and then purchase that amount of Ethereum. Both the Rainbow and MetaMask wallets discussed previously enable you to purchase crypto directly from your wallet. Coinbase Wallet requires you to acquire cryptocurrency from a different exchange and transfer it to your wallet.

Step 3: Link your wallet to an NFT Marketplace

After you have configured your wallet and acquired some ETH, it is time to find a marketplace on which to create an NFT and advertise your work. For those new to NFTs, I would recommend starting with Rarible, since the site had the simplest and most easy setup of any I tested.

To link your wallet to Rarible, navigate to the site and click the Connect icon in the upper right corner.

From the first minute you visit Rarible, the connect button is displayed.

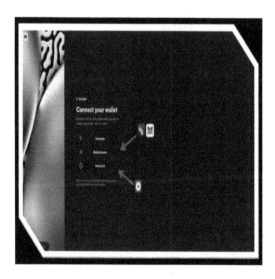

Select the WalletConnect option on the next page if you are using the Rainbow or Metamask wallets. If you are using Coinbase Wallet, click on WalletLink. Numerous other wallets are also supported by these connection options. Therefore, it is worthwhile to investigate each to see whether your favorite wallet is compatible.

Your connection method is determined by the wallet you are using.

Whichever wallet you are using, the following step is nearly same. Following your selection of a connecting method, a QR code will show on the screen. Scan this code with your wallet app. Once the code has been read, indicate that you want to link your wallet to Rarible.

To get started with Rarible, scan the QR code in your wallet app and press connect.

This is a secure connection, and Rarible will always need confirmation of purchases via your wallet app before proceeding. Your Rarible account is quickly created after linking a wallet. You now own all of the necessary components for creating, minting, and selling your first NFT.

Where can I sell NFTs?

New NFT markets are springing up on a regular basis as the technology's popularity grows. In this part, we will go through a few of the most popular online marketplaces and analyze how each one differs from the others, so you can make a better educated choice on where to offer your first NFT.

Zora

Zora is a marketplace founded on the principle that content creators should reclaim ownership of their work from big platforms. Creators can mint photos, movies, audio files, and even plain text documents using Zora. The marketplace is just launched, and it is now available to all creators.

Zora is already cooperating with prominent music artists like Toro y Moi, Mura Masa, and Yaeji, and is promoting itself as one of the trendiest locations for NFTs. We have also included a link to our own Kapwing Watermark.

Rarible

Rarible is one of the most user-friendly platforms for creators and collectors interested in NFTs. This was the first site I used when I originally began, and the platform makes submitting content and creating an NFT as easy as sharing a YouTube video. In a market dominated by invite-only platforms, Rarible is one of the few NFT platforms that enable new creators to begin selling their work as soon as they join up.

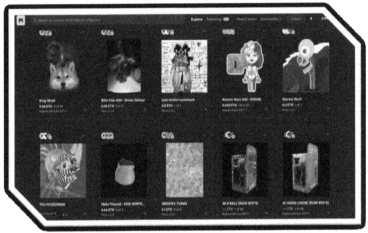

This openness results in a jumble of content on the site, and the service's monitoring of copyrighted and objectionable uploads should be better. Work on the site sells for a broad range of prices, from a few dollars to tens of thousands of dollars.

SuperRare

The NFT marketplace for digital artists is SuperRare's claim to fame. Memes, text postings, and basic sound effects are not for sale here. SuperRare's portfolio is carefully managed, and the company has taken a deliberate approach to onboarding new creators. As a consequence, viewing SuperRare is like entering an exclusive digital gallery.

The site has a wonderful collection of NFTs that represent hundreds of hours of work by artists. Prices may be rather high, and new creators are only approved after submitting an application.

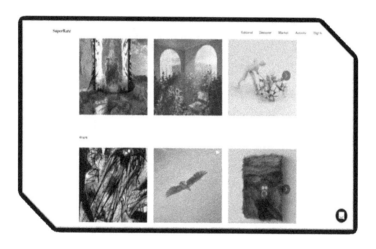

Nifty Gateway

Nifty Gateway is a carefully selected NFT marketplace that specializes on digital treasures. Nifty collaborates with high-profile artists and musicians such as Grimes and Justin Roiland to create limited-edition NFT collections. Nifty Gateway is one of the few prominent NFT sites that take credit cards, which sets it apart from the rest of the list. Nifty's art is often very pricey, and new artists must apply before they can submit work on the site, similar to SuperRare.

OpenSea

OpenSea has been one of the first NFT markets to be launched, and it offers a large library of content at a variety of rates. The site sells a wide range of NFTs, from digital art to 3D souvenirs and video game props. OpenSea is particularly welcoming to newcomers, making it simple to join. The site is quite user-friendly for people new to NFTs, and it features one of the greatest browsing experiences I have seen from a large marketplace. OpenSea is also the first NFT marketplace to publicly test a free creator creation method.

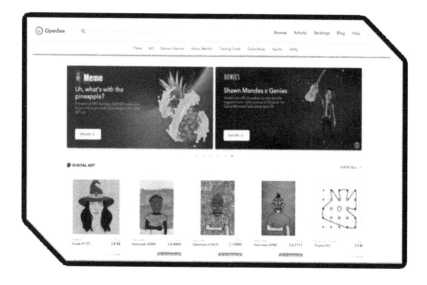

6.6 Uses of Token Standards

We examined a handful of widely used token contract standards in this chapter. What are these standards intended to accomplish? Should you abide by these rules? What are you going to do with them? Should you exceed these bare minimums? Which standards are you need to adhere to? Following that, we will examine some of those points.

How Are Token Requirements Defined?

What is their objective?

Token specifications are the very minimal standards for implementation. That is, to be compatible with, say, ERC20, you must at the very least implement the ERC20 standard's functions and behaviour. Additionally, you may enhance the functionality by implementing non-standard functions. These standards' principal objective is to facilitate contract interoperability.

Consequently, all wallets, exchanges, user interfaces, and other infrastructure components may predictably be with any contract that complies with the standard.

In other words, if you create an ERC20 contract, all existing wallet users will be able to trade your token without requiring them to upgrade their wallets or exert any effort on your behalf. The rules are descriptive rather than prescriptive.

It is entirely up to you to implement those functions; the contract's internal workings are unconnected to the standard. They contain certain functional requirements that regulate behaviour under specific circumstances, but they do not describe how they should be implemented. The behaviour of a transfer function when its value is set to zero illustrates this.

Should These Criteria Be Used?

With all of these standards in place, developers must choose between adhering to them and innovating outside the limits they impose. This is a challenging problem to resolve. Standards inherently constrain your freedom to create by imposing a constricting "rut" on which you must adhere.

On the other hand, the fundamental standards have evolved through experience with hundreds of applications and typically meet most use cases. This procedure also considers a far wider issue: the value of interoperability and widespread adoption. By implementing an established standard, you acquire the value of all the systems compatible with that standard.

Suppose you want to vary from the standard. In that case, you must factor in the expense of constructing all of the necessary support infrastructures yourself or convincing others to support your implementation as a new standard.

The "Not Invented Here" mentality, incompatible with open-source culture, refers to the propensity to build your path while disregarding established standards. On the other hand, creativity and development are contingent upon striking new ground.

Maturity brings with it a sense of security.

Apart from the standard, there is also an implementation alternative. When you choose to utilize a standard such as ERC20, you must next choose how to implement a compliant design. Various widely used "reference" implementations are available, or you may develop your own from scratch. Once again, this decision creates a problem with grave security consequences. Existing implementations have been "battle-tested" in the field.

While their security cannot be proven, several underpin tokens are valued millions of dollars. They have been frequently and vehemently assaulted. There have been no notable issues found so far. Writing your contract is challenging due to the myriad of subtle ways a contract can be violated. It is considerably safer to stick with a tried-and-true implementation.

In our examples, we utilized the OpenZeppelin implementation of the ERC20 standard since it is designed keeping security in mind from the start. Additionally, if you utilize an existing implementation, you may expand it.

Once again, go cautiously with this inclination. Complexity thwarts security. Each line of the code you write expands the attack surface of your contract and may represent an exploitable vulnerability. You may not detect an issue unless you exert considerable effort.

Standard Expansions for the Token Interface

The token standards discussed in this chapter provide a simple user interface with limited capability. Numerous projects have enhanced their implementations to meet the features required by their applications.

Among these features are the following:

Ownership authority

The ability to endow single addresses or groups of addresses with additional capabilities (i.e., multisignature schemes), such as blacklisting, whitelisting, minting, and recovery.

Burning

The capacity to destroy ("burn") tokens on purpose, either by moving them to an unspendable address or erasing a balance and lowering supply.

Minting

The ability to increase the overall quantity of tokens at a specified pace or using the creator's "fiat."

Crowdfunding

The ability to sell tokens by auction, market sale, or reverse auction, among other methods.

Recovery through backdoors

Functions to reverse transfers, recover funds, or deactivate the token that can be activated by a certain address or group of addresses.

Whitelisting

The ability to restrict activities to certain addresses (for example, token transfers). Most frequently, it is used to provide tokens to "accredited investors" after being verified following local regulations. Typically, there is a mechanism for maintaining the whitelist.

Blacklisting

The ability to restrict token transfers by specifying particular addresses to be excluded. Typically, a method is provided for updating the blacklist.

These numerous functions are implemented in reference libraries, such as the OpenZeppelin library. Several of them are case–sensitive and appear in only a few tokens. There are currently no widely agreed standards for these functions' interfaces. As previously stated, the option to extend a token standard's capabilities constitutes a trade-off between innovation and risk, as well as interoperability and security.

Tokens and Initial Coin Offerings

Tokens have become an increasingly important component of the Ethereum ecosystem. They are almost certain to become a necessary component of all smart contract platforms, including Ethereum. However, the relevance and potential influence of these standards should not be seen as an endorsement of present token offers.

As with early-stage technology, the initial wave of goods and firms will almost always fail, and some will fail miserably.

Numerous tokens accessible on Ethereum are glaringly evident frauds, pyramid schemes, and money grabs. The difficulty is to discern between the technology's long-term vision and influence, which are almost certain to be massive, and the short-term bubble of token ICOs, which is plagued with deception. Token standards and the platform will very certainly survive the current token bubble and then alter the course of human history.

In Ethereum, tokens are a strong notion that may serve as the foundation for many significant decentralized applications.

Conclusion

We appreciate your perseverance in reading this book to the finish; we hope it was educational and equipped you with the skills necessary to accomplish your objectives, whatever they may be. Simply finishing this book does not mean that you have mastered the subject; expanding your horizons is the only way to master the blockchain.

A distributed ledger enables cryptocurrencies to be audited regularly by an independent system known as the blockchain. The blockchain's concept is to use the collective intelligence of the population to verify and archive automatically. These nodes serve as the backbone of the blockchain network and provide a critical function.

Blockchain technology is still in its infancy. There is still a long way to go before we see the true power of the blockchain. Still, if the beginning is any indication, it is safe to say that the short-term benefits of incorporating the blockchain into a variety of other distributed technologies would be enormous.

Cryptocurrency has a skeptical reputation among people who do not understand it and others who see risk in it—whether actual or perceived. They frequently classify Bitcoin and the blockchain as illegal activities. I do not believe that for a moment. While privacy is the core of democracy, it has been gradually undermined in the name of security, and where have we ended up? Due to events such as advanced psychographic manipulation on social media and even large-scale surveillance by the powers that be, the blockchain has become the backbone of various diverse technologies; even IBM has begun to invest heavily in it. Cloud storage companies are looking at blockchain technologies to perfect distributed storage that is virtually impossible to destroy or hack.

The ideas are endless; consider a business combining the usefulness of distributed file storage with the adaptability of cryptocurrency to create a token. I bring this up to demonstrate how different blockchains may be.

The system's nodes form the blockchain, and each node associated contributes a fraction of its hard drive to the network. As a result, they keep some of their material on the network, secured by a blockchain. The blockchain taxes those who store data and then encrypts, splits, and distributes that data around the network. When a user wishes to retrieve it, he enters his private key and gains access to all his data, which is returned to him using BitTorrent technology.

To utilize this service, data must first acquire a cryptocurrency or token (such as Bitcoin) and then pay the service regularly with that token. Each time his hard drive space is utilized, the person who provides it receives a percentage of the revenue. The user automatically depletes his coin reserve as it is sent to the blockchain administrator and the nodes that store the data.

The money generated by the nodes is almost entirely automated and autonomous. They only need to keep their computer powered on, and the coin they pay for storage grows over time.

This example has a dual purpose. The first is to demonstrate the scalability and nature of blockchains; the second is to showcase the future wave of distributed applications created on top of blockchains and will operate in tandem with the token and coin markets.

The more the coin and token markets grow, the more Bitcoin advances. It appears that Bitcoin is the entrance point for many other cryptocurrencies, and the exchange market for these tokens and coins has grown extremely robust and shows no signs of slowing down.

Your interest in the blockchain, Bitcoin and Ethereum is likely based on sound intuition and should be fostered. You should take an early interest in this since it marks the beginning of a new era of business and money.

There are a few other areas to investigate if you intend to take this business seriously. You may wish to address certain concerns about cryptocurrency mining. There is a massive business out there that is still in its infancy. On the other side, if you are more of a trader and are not as knowledgeable about the technical parts of things, cryptocurrency trading may be interesting. Bitcoin trading has a lot of promise since it is a turbulent market. Program traders thrive in unpredictable markets because gains can be earned in either direction, and there are numerous arbitrage possibilities.

If mining and trading are not your things, but you work in other technology areas, you may want to consider an initial coin offering (ICO). Initial Coin Offerings, or ICOs, are a method of raising funds through the issuance of crypto-assets.

There are several areas in which you might invest to capitalize on the potential offered by this new industry of cryptocurrencies. You made an excellent choice by beginning with this book to understand the blockchain technology that underpins the crypto-asset.

Blockchains will revolutionize and transform the Internet. The signals are already in place, and all that is needed is time and ideas flow. The bigger institutional structures are collapsing in the face of blockchain technology, and its deployment will be nothing less than revolutionary. By the end of this century, the transition from centralized to decentralized architectures will be complete, and it will serve as the backbone of the Internet. It will also be the preferred method of deploying artificial intelligence, and the combination of AI, blockchains and the Internet of Things will define the future. Welcome in a new world!

This is especially true for the blockchain market, as it is a relatively new technology that is rapidly evolving. Only by developing a lifetime learning habit you can absorb it and use it to your advantage.

Whatever you do, bear in mind that the market is nearing an inescapable saturation point, which means that regardless of how you engage with blockchain technology, you must ensure that you come out on the winning side.

It is extremely unlikely that you will see another disruptive technology in your lifetime. With so many technology variants and cryptocurrencies vying for market share simultaneously, all you need to do is to recognize the possibility of success to seek it out and reap the associated benefits.

This also implies that there are multiple ways to fail, which means that you must do your due diligence and never take action without examining all of your choices first. Bear in mind that investing in blockchain technology is a long-term endeavor; patience and persistence always pays off.

www.ingramcontent.com/pod-product-compliance
Lightning Source LLC
Chambersburg PA
CBHW051055050326
40690CB00006B/728